Mommy Help Me

By
Shaquana Jackson

Copyright © 2015 by Shaquana N. Jackson all rights reserved.

This book or any portion thereof may not be reproduced or used in any manner whatsoever without the express written permission of the publisher except for the use of brief quotations in a book review

Printed in the United States of America

First Printing, 2016

ISBN
Sophisticated Real-Life Publications
P.O. Box 988
Abbeville, La 70511
www.shaquanajackson.com

Table Of Contents

Chapter One 4

Chapter Two 11

Chapter Three 18

Chapter Four 28

Chapter Five 45

Chapter Six 60

Chapter Seven 79

Chapter Eight 102

Chapter Nine 144

Chapter Ten 173

Chapter One

Anita was in the kitchen cooking when Aniya entered through the doorway. Aniya tossed her book bag by the kitchen table before walking up to her mother.

"Hi, momma," Aniya said.

Aniya was Anita's sixteen-year-old daughter.

"Don't 'momma' me. Where were you today? Because you sure weren't at school!" Anita returned in a furiously tone, putting her knife down and turning towards Aniya.

"I was at school momma," replied Aniya.

"What have I told you about that lying?" Anita said in a deep, hotly tone.

Aniya stood still without saying a word, breathing hard as if she were running.

"Now, I told you about having those white folks call my house telling me how I'm a 'downright no-good mother' in their book," said Anita, walking up to her daughter. "You still don't understand what I mean about putting those white folks in my business! Calling me like I can't raise my own child!" Anita pointed her finger in Aniya's face with rage.

"Maybe they're right! You care more about your drugs than me anyway!" Aniya retorted before her mother slapped her right across the face.

Aniya quickly grabbed her face with one hand.

"Don't you ever talk that way to me! Whatever I do is my business, and as long as you're under my roof you will do exactly what I say. Is that understood?"

Aniya did not say a word.

"Child, are you testing me?" Anita asked, getting closer to Aniya's face.

"It won't happen again," Aniya said.

"Good. Now go to your room and do your homework or something. Food is almost ready."

Aniya picked up her book bag cautiously before walking to her room, momentarily looking back at her mom. She flopped on her bed with her headphones on and her eyes closed.

She fell asleep.

***

As Anita walked into her daughter's bedroom, she found her asleep on the bed. With a huff, Anita walked over to Aniya's bed and pulled the headphones out of her ears.

She woke up immediately.

"Don't you think it's time to get up and take a bath? You have school tomorrow. Did you even get any of your homework questions done?"

Aniya sleeplessly looked at the homework sheets that was spread across her bed. "I don't have that much, I will get to it." Aniya replied.

"I know you will. I'm about to leave, I have to make a run—so pick up after you finish that homework."

"Again…" Aniya mumbled.

"Come again?"

"Okay."

"Come lock the door behind me," Anita said, exiting Aniya's room.

"Yeah," Aniya agreed as she got up off the bed and followed her mother.

"Give me a kiss," Anita said.

Aniya leaned over and kissed her mother goodbye.

"I love you," said Anita.

"Yeah, yeah, sure," said Aniya.

"Will I ever get a decent reply out of you regardless of what I do? I still make a way for us."

There's silence as Aniya looked her mother dead in the eye, "I love you too, mom."

"Well good, now that's my baby," Anita said. She quickly kissed her daughter on the forehead and wrapped her arms around her and squeezed her tight.

***

Aniya was in her bedroom doing some homework questions when she heard a knock on her window. Putting down her papers, she walked over to the window, pulled it open, and looked outside.

That was when she realized who it was.

"Hey Malik, what are you doing here?" she asked eagerly.

"Hey beautiful, open the door," he said as his lips turned into a grin.

Aniya smiled back and moved out of her room to go to the front door. She pulled the chain off the door before letting Malik into her home.

Malik didn't hesitate to kiss her.

"Wow, what was that for?" she asked.

"Just for being the most beautiful and smartest girl that ever walked the Earth."

"Oh, someone must be in a good mood—and knows the right thing to say." Aniya returned playfully. "Do you care for something to eat?"

"Sure."

"Come on, my mom just cooked."

***

Later that evening, Aniya and Malik walked to the club. They snuck in from time to time together. They got past the bouncer with no trouble at all, and no one seemed to notice them the several hours they were there.

"Hey, I'm glad you had fun, we need to do this more often," said Malik.

"What, sneak into clubs and drink?" Aniya retorted with a giggle.

"It was fun, you have to admit."

"Yes, I must agree."

They held hands as they walked down the dark sidewalk. "These will be memories for us, Bonnie and Clyde," Malik said as he put his arms around Aniya's waist.

But just then, a car slowly pulled up to the side of Aniya and Malik, seemingly out of nowhere. As the car stopped, Aniya stopped walking as well. "Oh boy."

This couldn't be anything but trouble.

The car door opened, and Malik looked equally stunned. "'Oh boy' is right."

"Malik, get your ass in this car. This what you do? Sneak around with hookers all night and think you're going to come into my house anytime you want?" The woman inside the car looked furious.

"But momma—"

"Don't 'momma' me nothing. I'm gonna make you sorry in front of whoever she is," Malik's mom said, flinging her hand in front Aniya's face as if she was nothing.

"Mom, she is not a hooker and that's not a way to judge somebody you don't even know. Now would you please give her a ride?"

"First off, for a girl as young as she is to be hanging in the streets this time of the night, she's either tricking or up to no good," she said before getting cut off by Malik.

"Please Ma," he pleaded.

"Please nothing, because I'm not through with you either," she said as she placed one hand on her hip. "And besides, I don't let trash get in my car—and she is not my child. How she got here is how she can get home before you mess around and catch a charge."

"Look, I don't have to take this from someone who does not know how to do anything but disrespect me. I haven't done anything to you," Aniya responded before she stormed off.

"I'm sorry, are you going to be okay?" Malik asked as he caught up with Aniya and gently pulled her by the arm to turn her around.

"I'll be fine," Aniya said as she continued to walk, pulling her arm away from Malik.

Aniya began down a dark alleyway as a howling wind sent gusts down the path. Trash was blowing about in every single direction.

Aniya began to pick up her speed when she heard something—or someone—behind her. She quickly turned around, but spotted no one. Aniya took a deep breath in relief.

She continued to walk faster until someone touched her shoulder. Aniya jumped while letting out a horrific scream. She turned around quickly.

"Hey, do you have a dollar?" A bum asked her. He had raggedy clothes and a face painted with dirt.

Aniya covered her nose due to his horrible smell, which covered the whole block. "No, leave me alone!" She shouted in fear.

Aniya looked up as she turned the corner and there was the sound of sirens as several cops jumped out of their cars with guns in their hands. They stopped just across the street from Aniya as people came running out of an abandoned building with broken windows and graffiti covering most of its exterior.

Aniya watched in awe as she folded her arms tightly to protect herself from the harsh winds. She witnessed a cop smash a lady to the ground, and the others handcuffing even more people.

Police were shouting: "Put your hands behind your back." While others were holding their guns and screaming: "Get down, get down!"

"Ah gosh, that must hurt," Aniya whispered to herself as the cop lifted the lady up by her one handcuffed hand.

The lady looked sadly in Aniya's direction.

Aniya stared at the lady as the lady stared at her. It was like time paused for just a moment. Aniya put her hand to her mouth when she finally recognized the lady.

"Mom," she whispered, as tears flowed down her face.

Her mother just shook her head, as if in warning. The cop then shoved her into the police car and slammed the door shut.

Anita stared at Aniya from inside the window.

"Mommy!" Aniya cried.

Chapter Two

It was 8:30 a.m. when Aniya woke up to a knock on her door. She picked herself up off of the floor before wandering over to the living room door.

The knock hit once more.

Aniya opened the door and couldn't get a word out before the guest started talking.

"Hello, my name is Mrs. Shirley. I'm your mother's—" she was cut off by Aniya.

"I know who you are," Aniya replied heatedly.

"Is your mother home?" Mrs. Shirley asked.

"No, she isn't."

"Well, here, take my card. Tell her to call me as soon as possible. If I don't hear from her by next week—with her payment—her insurance will relapse."

"Sure," said Aniya indifferently. Before she shut the door.

Aniya walked into the kitchen and rubbed her stomach. She opened the refrigerator and spotted nothing but an empty carton of milk and some moldy cheese.

She closed the refrigerator and went over to the sink. She rinsed her glass before filling it with water.

Opening the cabinet, she noticed a box of crackers and reached for them. She quickly began wolfing them down, washing them down with the glass of water.

Just then, the phone rang.

Aniya picked the phone from the receiver.

"You have a collect call from Anita," said an automated voice.

Aniya quickly answered, "Yes."

"Mom."

"Hi honey, I'm so glad you're not at school, or I would have been in a major jam."

"Really can't believe you're saying that, mother. You know those white folks will call you again," Aniya said sarcastically.

"Look Aniya, this is not the time," her mother replied seriously.

"Well what do you expect? I watched my mom being handcuffed and thrown into a cop car, and I'm supposed to go to school as if everything is okay? Mom, what happened?"

"Listen, I will explain that later, what I need you to do is look in my room, in my closet, and open the shoe box to the left. Take that money and get a cab to take you downtown, go to the shadow apartment to apartment B."

"What will I do there?"

"Just listen Aniya, I don't have all day on this phone!" Anita shouted.

"Okay already."

"There's a guy name Craig that lives there. Tell him to come bail me out, please."

"Sure. Momma, do you have extra money so I can get something to eat? I'm starving."

"No, dammit, that's all I have! You will eat when I get out!" she huffed. "I love you."

Aniya hung up.

"Yeah right, if you loved me, you would be here for your only child and stop putting me though these rough times!"

***

Aniya found the money and stepped onto the street to stop a taxi.

"Downtown please," Aniya said as her eyes shifted from the interior of the taxi to the apartment buildings that surrounded her.

As the car rolled to a stop, Aniya paid the taxi driver and got out of the car.

"Wow, what a beautiful apartment complex," she said as she stared in awe. Aniya looked around until she spotted apartment B. She stepped up to the apartment, pushed her hair back, and rang the doorbell.

No one came to the door.

She decided to knock.

When no one came to the door, she took a deep breath and started to walk away. It was then that someone opened the door. Aniya quickly turned around.

The tall, brown skinned man wore a two-piece red suit with white stripes, and a frown upon his face. He stared at her without saying a word, placing an unlit cigar in his mouth.

"Uh, hello. My name is Aniya," she said nervously. She smiled shyly, fidgeting with her fingers. The man continued to stare. "You must be Craig," she offered.

Craig took the cigar out of his mouth. "And you are?" he asked with a grin upon his face, leering at her.

"I'm Anita's daughter."

Craig's eyes got big and his grin disappeared. It was as if he'd seen a ghost. "Really?" He asked, licking his lips.

There was silence as Aniya nodded her head.

"Come on in," he offered.

Aniya slowly stepped into the apartment while looking around. There were nice, artistic photos of African American people, trophies throughout the living room, leather couches, and nice fancy rugs. It was beautifully coordinated.

"You have a really nice place," she complimented while smiling.

"Well thank you. Have a seat," he said as his eyes continued to follow Aniya's body.

"Thanks."

"May I get you a drink?"

"Yes, I would love that. Do you have a coke?"

"Well I can tell you that's one thing you got from Anita. But she liked her coke mixed with liquor," he said with a giggle.

"Yeah, that's my mom's favorite soda," she said with a chuckle.

"I'll get it for you," Craig said as he exited the living room and went to the kitchen.

"Okay, thanks," she said, as she continued sitting on the couch, looking in the opposite direction. Craig licked his lips as she watched Aniya from afar. Aniya got off the sofa and looked around at all the pictures and trophies on the wall and on the shelves.

"Here you go," said Craig. Aniya jumped when she turned to notice Craig standing right behind her.

"Thanks," Aniya said, nervously grabbing her drink from Craig as she slowly walked away from him.

Craig continued to stare at Aniya. "Well, the reason for me being here is because my mom is in jail, and she needs you to bail her out."

"Is that right? What did Ms. Anita do now?" Craig said in a deep tone as he shook his head, unsurprised.

"She said you can go bail her out at the station," Aniya said, trying to ignore the question he had asked. Craig dug in his pocket and pulled out a roll of money.

Aniya's eyes got big as she stared at the money, tucking her hair behind her ear. Silence filled the room as Aniya took a complimentary sip of coke.

"Here," Craig said as he took the rubber band off of his money and passed some out to Aniya. Aniya just stared. "Well, aren't you going to take it?" he asked as he put the money in front of Aniya's face.

"Oh, I'm too young to bail out my mom."

Craig let out a loud giggle. "Is something funny, Mr. Craig? Because it looks like I missed it." Aniya said with aggravation.

"Get some food, clothes, or your hair fixed or something. There's no reason for a young lady as beautiful as yourself to be looking the way you do."

Aniya stood there in silence and confusion. Was it supposed to be a blessing to have the money offered to her—or was he insulting her? Aniya slowly reached for the money, but Craig pulled it back.

"Nuh uh, what will you give me?" Craig asked as he moved closer to Aniya and ran his fingers through her hair.

"Get your hands out of my hair!" Aniya shouted as she pushed Craig's hand away from her.

"Don't get smart with me, you came to me for help," Craig said as he suddenly pulled Aniya's head back by pulling her hair.

"Ouch. Let me go, you creep!"

Craig reached to kiss her lips as she fell back on the sofa, fighting to get away.

"Stop! Stop!" Aniya continued to scream while swinging her fists at Craig. Craig got on top of Aniya as she screamed for help. He then covered Aniya's mouth as he pushed up her shirt roughly.

Someone knocked on the door.

"Hey Craig, you in here?" A guy asked as he slowly opened Craig's door, continuing to knock. "Craig," the guy said as he saw Craig tussling with her on the couch.

Aniya took the opportunity to push Craig off of her as she quickly got up, pulling down her shirt. "He tried to rape me!" Aniya cried to the unknown guy as he stood in silence.

Craig slapped Aniya across the face and threw the money at her as she hit the floor. Aniya continued to cry even louder as she got off the floor, so quickly that she left the money right where it landed and dashed out the front door.

"Slut!" Craig shouted as he watched Aniya leave his home.

***

Anita and Aniya were both in the living room picking up when Anita spoke up. "What took you so long? You can never do anything in a timely manner," she said with rage before Aniya cut her off.

"I'm sorry momma, no need to shout at me. I got to that creep Craig's house as soon as I could," Aniya said as she picked a beer can off of the floor.

"You don't speak that way about a man who has given me money when I didn't have it to feed you," Anita said, getting in Aniya's face. Aniya just stared her mother in the eye.

"What were you behind bars for this time?" Aniya said fiercely.

"Look," Anita said as she took a frustrated breath, pointing her finger in Aniya's face. "I don't have to explain anything to you. However," she took a deep breath and put down her hand. "I was in the wrong place at the wrong time." Anita said abruptly as she scratched her head while staring into Aniya's eyes.

Anita quickly changed the subject. "The question is: what were you doing out of the house at that time of the night, missy? All by yourself. Someone could have hurt you, or something bad could have happened," she said, placing her hands on her hips.

Aniya puts her head down.

"Look at me when I'm talking to you, child."

"I just went for a walk to look for you," Aniya said as a nervous sweat beaded on her forehead. It was obvious she was deceitful.

"You have no reason to look for me. I am grown. You could have gotten hurt in those streets. It is very dangerous for young girls to be out that time of the night. Now this better not happen again, is that understood?

Aniya just nodded.

Chapter Three

The next day, Aniya was walking down a noisy hall at school. Kids were chatting with one another and a boyfriend and girlfriend were making out on the lockers. Aniya walked to her locker when she took notice of Malik hugged up with another girl just a few lockers from hers.

Her eyes were big and she took a deep breath as she stormed off towards Malik. "What is going on here?"

"Baby, hi," Malik said as he reached over to give her a kiss. Aniya quickly backed away as she folded her arms.

"What is going on?" she asked again angrily.

"Look, calm down. This is Shania, a new girl that just moved to my block. This is her first day here at our school." He was trying to keep his cool.

"So you hugged her why?" Aniya asked as she unfolded her arms and placed them on her hips instead.

"Well, that looks like my cue. Thanks again Malik, I got it from here," Shania said as she walked off, looking Aniya up and down.

"Would you please fix that face? It is not what it seems Aniya, you're the only girl for me and you know that," Malik said as he kissed her on the cheek.

"I'm sorry, I don't know what got into me. I just made myself look like a fool, huh?" she said with her head down and her arms folded as she swayed from side to side.

"You're fine," he said as he pulled her into a hug.

"So, what are we going to do after school?" Aniya asked.

"I have football practice."

"We can do something after that," Aniya offered.

"No, I'm afraid I have a meeting with the coach. I am getting a scholarship and this is my last year, so we have to get everything situated before I graduate. I might be busy for quite some time."

"You say it like you have no worries in the world, Malik. I mean, what happens to us after graduation?"

"Look, not here, not now. We'll discuss this later, "he said before walking off.

"Malik! Malik!" Aniya called.

She took a deep breath as she walked to her class alone. Aniya walked into her classroom late and everyone stared at her. "Stop right there," Mrs. Trahan said as she looked at Aniya. Aniya stopped with a confused look on her face. "What did I tell you about coming to my class late?" Mrs. Trahan said, folding her arms while standing in front of the classroom.

"I'm only two minutes late." Aniya said.

"I don't care if you're a minute late, Miss. Aniya. This has occurred on more than one occasion and I just won't allow it. Not for you or any of my other students," Mrs. Trahan said with a quick pause. "You'll get a warning now, but I will have a note sent home calling for a parent-teacher meeting, is that understood?"

"There's no need for that. I promise this will be my last time," Aniya begged.

"Yes, you said that last time, and the time before. I cannot let this slide any longer. I want to meet with your parents. Is that understood, little girl?"

"Yes," Aniya said as she put her head down.

"Yes what?" Mrs. Trahan asked.

"Yes, ma'am."

"Much better. Now have a seat."

***

After school Aniya was walking alone behind three girls on the sidewalk.

"Oh my god, look at that crack head over there," one of the girls said, causing the other two to burst out laughing.

"Looks like she's had those clothes on for days!" said one of the other girls.

"Yeah, she's harassing one of the biggest drug dealers hoping he might throw her something just because he feels sorry for her," replied the third girl as they continued to laugh.

Aniya turned to notice that the crack head the girls were referring to was none other than her mother, begging from a man known as the biggest drug dealer in the neighborhood. Aniya began walking faster, turning her head in shame so as to not to let anyone know that was her mother.

Having been so concerned with her mother, Aniya accidentally bumped into one of the girls ahead of her. "Hey, like, could you watch where you going, geek?"

"I'm sorry, it was an accident," Aniya said as she continued to walk with her hand over her face.

Aniya made it home when she suddenly stopped walking and stared at her halfway-opened door. Aniya slowly walked through the door. "Hello? Is someone in here?"

No answer.

"What happened here?" Aniya demanded as she noticed the trash and the broken vase on the floor. She heard a noise from the kitchen and jumped.

More curious than before, Aniya slowly walked to the kitchen. There was the sound of something hitting the inside of the bottom cabinet. Aniya stared at the cabinet in fear, before slowly opening it. She let out a scream when a cat came flying out—knocking her to the floor.

She put her hand over her heart as she breathed heavily. "Okay, calm down Aniya. It's just a cat," she said to herself.

She walked into the living room to find Malik standing there with his hands behind his back.

"Malik! Hey, you scared me!" Aniya said with an awkward smile on her face— she was always happy to see him, but not at that particular time.

"Listen, I'm sorry for getting upset earlier. I was being sort of a jerk," he said gently.

"Sort of a jerk?" Aniya responded sarcastically.

"Anyhow, I got this for you," he said, pulling a bouquet of flowers out from behind his back.

"Ah thanks, you shouldn't have," Aniya said as she took the flowers and smelled them. "I'll put them in a vase. I'm so ashamed; I don't know what happened to this place. I came home and this is how I found it."

"It's okay, I'm not here to judge you," Malik said. "I'll help you clean up, then we can go to the burger joint and get something to eat."

"Wow Malik, just when I think you can't surprise me anymore! It sounds great," she said with a smile.

Mommy Help Me

***

Malik and Aniya were at the burger joint, laughing and chatting away. "Look, I'm really loving you, and I'm sorry for the way I've been acting lately—it's just a lot of stress with my mom and the college stuff, but it's no reason for to be treating you any differently," he said as he put his hand on top of hers.

Aniya smiled.

Malik looked up when some company stopped by their table. "Hey, my favorite girl!" Malik said as he smiled up at his little sister. She was looking as dazzling as ever with her natural, long wavy hair, her cut up blue jeans, and a nice sweater top.

"Hey big brother," Coretta said. "So when are you going to be ready? You know momma doesn't want you late to your own party."

"Nice to see you again, Malik," said Shania, the new girl, who had on a black leather mini skirt, a short top, and red boots.

"Likewise," said Malik.

Aniya moved her hand away from Malik's. "Look, me and Shania will go get ourselves together. You know we have to round up all the cheerleaders—it will be a party you won't forget, I promise big bro."

"Fa sho, I'll catch up with ya'll in a minute."

Aniya put her head down as Coretta and Shania walked away without saying a word to her.

"Look baby—" Malik said before Aniya interrupted him.

"A party, wow. That's nice. You weren't going to let me know anything about it, like it wasn't going to get out!" Aniya said as she got up from the table.

"Wait!" Malik begged as he grabbed her by the wrist.

"Even the new girl is invited. Wow Malik, you didn't even have the heart to tell me. That really hurts."

"Baby, you know how my mom is with you and it's at her house," he said.

"Right, I get it. I'm just a horrible girl from around the way," Aniya snapped as she snatched her wrist out of his hand. Malik watched Aniya as she stormed out of the fast food joint.

***

Aniya made it home when she noticed her mother was passed out on the sofa. Her shirt was halfway up, showing some of her bra, and her hair was all over the place. She walked over to her mother.

"Momma, momma," Aniya said as she tapped her mother on the shoulder.

"Yeah, what is it Aniya? I can't ever get any rest around here—if it ain't one thing, it's another," Anita mumbled as she turned over.

"Well, if you'd be home as much as you hang out in the streets, you would be able to rest just fine," Aniya responded bluntly.

"Aniya, I told you about playing with me, little girl!" Anita shouted as she jumped up off the sofa. "I don't know what's come over you Aniya, but you better lay off with the mouth, or I will deck you one right across those smart lips of yours!"

"You have to go to school tomorrow to speak with one of my teachers," Aniya blurted out.

"What did you do Aniya?" Anita questioned. "You're always messing up, Aniya. I can't keep running to solve your problems, saving you every time you mess up."

"I wonder where I get it from. Besides, what are you here for? You're sure not a mother. Mother's help their children, that's what mother's do," Aniya said before she stormed off to her room.

***

At Malik's party, there were blue and white decorations throughout the living room and the kitchen. His sister, Coretta, was dressed in a white tank top with blue short shorts. Coretta answered the door, letting the football players in. Some people were dancing and singing along to the music while others were snacking and drinking punch. Malik was still in the bathroom getting dressed.

Coretta knocked on the bathroom door. "If you stay in there a little longer, you will miss your own party," she stated sarcastically.

"I'll be out in just a second."

"Okay hurry, everyone is here."

Music was playing as Sandra finished putting the icing on his cake. Malik finally came down and greeted his team.

Just then, the doorbell rang.

Coretta answered the door. "Hi Shania, glad you could make it, girl!" Coretta said in a cheerful tone.

"Me too! I had to plead with my folks, and you know how that is," Shania replied as she and Coretta hugged.

Everyone was having a good time dancing and chatting away when Shania walked into the living room. All the football players stopped what they were doing to greet her. Shania just smiled as she made her way to Malik.

"Hi Malik," she said.

"What's up? Glad you could make it," Malik responded, rubbing his head nervously as sweat appeared across his forehead.

"Yeah, me too." Shania said flirtatiously, moving her hips from side to side to the beat of the music.

"Okay everyone, food is done! If you're hungry, meet me in the kitchen!" Sandra called.

Everyone rushed into the kitchen except for Malik and Shania. "So are you hungry?" Malik asked her.

"Yeah, sure," said Shania.

"Well, after you," Malik replied.

Everyone was enjoying themselves and having a nice time. Malik took off to his room and shut his door behind him. He picked up his cellphone as he dialed a number. After a few rings he got impatient and hung up his phone. Malik put down his phone and turned around, only to see Shania standing there.

"I hope I didn't scare you," Shania said, standing with one hand on her hip.

"No, not at all."

It got quiet.

"Look Malik, I know it's kind of awkward that—"

"Hey, don't even worry about it. The past is the past," Malik said as he placed his phone on the dresser.

"Look Malik, I didn't have a choice. We were just kids and we had to travel with my daddy's job," she said as she sat down on his bed.

"You don't have to explain anything to me. What was done was done, even though my heart was pulled out of my chest when you left," Malik said as he placed his hand over his heart in a joking manner.

Shania smiled. "Am I making you nervous?" she asked, watching Malik pace back and forth across the room, fidgeting with his hands as sweat appeared on his forehead once more.

Malik smirked as he wiped the sweat off of his forehead. "So that means I do make you nervous," Shania said as she got off the bed and approached Malik.

"No, you don't make me nervous. I just have a lot on my mind, that's all."

"Well, you need me to help ease your mind," Shania said as she leaned closer. She kissed Malik once on the lips. "We're a little bit older now."

Malik began to enjoy the kisses as they fell onto his bed.

"Malik?" Coretta called as she opened his bedroom door. She found Malik on top of Shania. "Ooh, my bad," she said with a smile.

Malik quickly jumped up as Shania sat up. "It's not what you think."

"Oh no big bro, you don't have to explain yourself to me. I'll just go back to the party like I don't know anything," Coretta teased while closing the door.

Malik's cell phone began to ring. "I better get that," he said.

"Why don't you answer that later and we can go back and enjoy your party? Shania said with a smile. Malik winked as he walked to his door, looking back for Shania to follow him.

"I'll just freshen up and I'll meet you in a bit," Shania said, twirling her hair.

"Do your thing," Malik agreed with a smile before he closed the door behind him.

Shania grabbed Malik's phone off of the dresser and opened it. "Oh, it's from you, Aniya. I'll just erase it. I'm back and pretty soon you'll be out the way. I promise he won't even remember your name," Shania said to herself. A smirk played at her lips as she put the phone back where she found it.

Chapter Four

Aniya woke up the next morning to find her mother in the kitchen cooking breakfast.

"Good morning," Anita said as she continued to scramble the eggs.

"Morning," Aniya returned with a surprised look on her face, wondering if it was a holiday she forgot about. Where did this food come from?

Aniya kissed her mom on the cheek. "Look mom, I'm sorry for what I said yesterday. I didn't mean it."

"It's okay. You know, sometimes I deserve that. I'm not the mother I should be at times," her mother responded as she turned off the burner. "You know, it's hard fighting this drug addiction. I feel like I can't live if I don't have it..." she said, her voice cracking. "I'm sorry for putting you through all this mess of mine," she admitted as tears rolled down her eyes.

"It's okay mom, and besides, I'm not making it any easier for you with my unwanted comments and my behavior," Aniya noted as she hugged her mother tight. Tears rolled down Aniya's face as well.

"I love you Aniya, no matter what. I love you from the bottom of my heart," her mother said as tears continued to flow heavily down her cheek.

"I love you too momma, you're all I have. You're all I have," Aniya agreed. Teardrops fell from her eyes.

***

Aniya and Anita were in the conference room at Aniya's school.

"I'm sorry to have you take time out of your busy schedule Ms. Cooper, but Miss. Aniya here has been late for my class on many occasions. This disrupts the class and interferes with their learning," Mrs. Trahan explained.

"I'm sorry this has been taking place, but I will make sure to have a long talk with my daughter to make sure this does not happen again," Anita responded.

"I must say, she's a very smart girl. She keeps all her grades up no matter what. She will become something great in her future," Mrs. Trahan added.

"Sometimes I don't know how she does it, but she does," Anita said as she put her head down.

"Maybe it's because she has a good mother like you," Mrs. Trahan offered.

"I don't know about that," Anita mumbled as she picked up her head with a fake smile.

"She is a good kid. However, she will be in in-school suspension. If she does well, she will be back in her regular class the following day. If she gives trouble, she will be in outer school suspension, which requires her to stay home. But I doubt it will get to that. Do we have any questions?"

"She will straighten up. There will be no more problems," Anita assured.

"Thank you for your time."

"You're welcome."

Her mother and her teacher both rose from their seats at the same time, shaking hands. Anita left, but Aniya stayed in place. As Mrs. Trahan stood and walked around her, she put her arms around Aniya's shoulders and led her back to class.

In the hallway, Mrs. Trahan and Aniya approached Malik. "Hi there Malik, I heard you were being accepted in South Boston University. That's one of the best colleges around and many scouts are always looking out for new talent there on that football field—congrats," she said as she hugged Malik.

"Thanks Mrs. Trahan, that means a lot coming from my favorite teacher," Malik said with a smile.

"You always knew how to make your favorite teacher smile," Mrs. Trahan responded with a giggle.

"Aniya," Malik started, but Aniya walked off to her class as if she didn't hear a word.

The bell rang as Aniya and Malik both exited their classroom and walked outside separately.

"Hey Aniya, how long will you keep playing this game?" Malik asked, grabbing her by the arm.

"Let me go. I'm not the one who's playing games," she huffed.

Coretta and Shania were walking outside when they stopped to watch Aniya and Malik from a distance.

"Look, I'm sorry I didn't tell you about the stupid party. It wasn't fun anyway. There, you happy?" he grumbled as he let go of her arm.

"It wasn't?" Aniya replied, though it was more of a question.

"No, because you weren't there."

"Ah, you're just saying that to try and make me feel better. Try again."

"No, I'm serious Aniya."

"Why didn't you answer the phone when I called you, Malik? If it wasn't so fun?"

"You never called me," Malik stated with a confused look on his face.

"Look, if you don't believe me, look at my phone," Aniya said before handing her phone over to Malik. Malik took a look at the call log.

"I'm sorry baby, I don't know what happened. I didn't see a missed call from you," he explained as he handed the phone back over to Aniya. "You have to let me make this up to you."

Aniya sighed in frustration.

Coretta and Shania walked up. "Hey big bro, you care to give your sister and a friend a ride home?"

"Of course lil sis."

"Hi girls," Aniya greeted.

"Aniya," Coretta acknowledged.

"Hi," Shania returned shortly, swinging her hair to the left side of her shoulder.

"By the way, I have to tell you Malik, your party was so off the chain—I just hope it's not the last. I'm sure your mom will put another one on for you as soon as you graduate," Shania said flirtatiously as she put her hands on her hips.

Aniya's smile slowly dropped from her face.

"Oh fa sho, fa sho, maybe one more before I depart," Malik said with a chuckle as a blush formed on his face.

"Well, me and Shania will be in the car waiting for you," Coretta said as the girls walked off.

Malik continued to watch them as they walked away.

"Don't stare too hard, you might hurt yourself," Aniya said before she walked off. Malik grabbed her arm gently.

"Look, stop with all that pouting. How about I take you out tonight on a date? What do you say about that? Just me and you," he said with as he winked his eye.

"I'll think about it."

"'I'll think about it,'" Malik echoed in mockery.

"Come here, my favorite girl," Malik said as he put his arm around Aniya's waist. They walked off together.

***

Night fell as Malik walked Aniya home.

"Why do you keep looking back? Are you running away from the law and I don't know about it?" Malik joked.

"Actually yes. Officer Sandra," Aniya joked as she and Malik laughed.

"Okay, I see someone's got jokes tonight about my mom being an officer, right?"

"Well she was always sneaking up on us and giving me the third degree. And she takes your car away every time she thinks you're coming to see me."

"All right, not true."

"Is that so?"

Malik stopped walking and smiled at Aniya. "I want to give you something," he said, biting his lip.

"What?" Aniya stopped in her tracks, continuing to smile from ear to ear.

Malik pulled a tiny box from his pocket. Immediately, Aniya put her hand over her chest as she began breathing heavily. Malik opened the box and she stared in awe at the gold ring with a diamond in the middle.

"Malik," Aniya said. Malik took the ring out of the box before gently taking her hand.

"This is a promise ring," Malik began while staring into Aniya's eyes. "I promise to always love you and never leave your side, no matter what." he said while sliding the ring on her finger. "Even if I'm away at college, you will still be close to me because I promise to carry you in my heart."

"Malik, how sweet. I love it. And I almost love you the same," Aniya joked as she hugged him.

As Aniya and Malik stopped hugging, Malik noticed Aniya's smile was no longer there. "What's wrong baby?"

"It's just, you know," she began as she took a short pause. "You will be gone soon, and then what? I mean I won't have you around anymore. No one to talk to or to confide in," she said while staring at her new ring.

"Hey," Malik said as he raised her head, putting his hand under her chin. "I will be here some weekends, and holidays. I will be around and before you know it, time will fly and you'll graduate and we can live happily ever after," he said with one of his sexy smiles.

"Sounds beautiful," she said as she hugged Malik once more.

"There's something else I have for you."

"What is it?"

"Come, it's a surprise," Malik said as he held Aniya's hand, guiding her.

"Malik, this is your house," she said, confused.

"You've won a million dollars."

"Stop kidding around."

"Come on, I've got a surprise for you."

"You know your mom doesn't like me. I am not putting one foot in that house," Aniya said as she placed her hand on her hip.

"No one is here, stop being a party pooper," Malik said as he followed Aniya into the house.

Aniya and Malik made it into his room.

"Wow, you have a cool room, and it's beautiful—did you do this for me?" Aniya said as she noticed the rose petals on the bed and the candles lit.

"Of course my love, who else would I do this for? Here, let me take your jacket."

"Sure," she said as she turned around. "It's a shame it took you this long to take me here. I don't mean your room, but to your house period."

"I'm sorry, Aniya."

"No Malik, it's like you're scared to stand up to your mother. Scared to let her know I'm the one you love and that I'm not a bad person. You're scared to see exactly what it is that's keeping her from getting to know me."

"Well, soon enough she will see that, Aniya. Listen, I don't want to bicker tonight," he said, taking a deep breath. "I want this night to be special, that's all. Now come here," he said as he pulled Aniya to him and took a seat on his bed. "I want you to understand that you mean everything to me. Since I will be going soon, I thought this night should be special for us. Now come here and give me a kiss," he said as he pulled Aniya in the bed with him while kissing her gently.

***

At 12:00 a.m. Aniya quietly sneaked back to her house while trying to fix her hair. She slowly closed the front door and locked it. She crept into the lit kitchen when she noticed her mom and a strange guy getting high at the kitchen table.

"Mom, what are you doing?" Aniya shouted.

Anita quickly put down the crack pipe as she stared at her daughter. The strange guy continued to hit the pipe.

"Aniya, what are you doing just coming in the house at this time of the night? I thought you were in bed!"

"Mom, is this what you like to do? Get high all the time?"

"You don't worry about what I do. I'm grown and this is my house. Now go to your room before I slap you for walking in my house at this time of night, thinking that you can continue to do what you want to do!" she said as she turned away from Aniya.

"What kind of example are you? Getting high and bringing strangers in the house all times of the night?"

Anita quickly picked up a chair and threw it at Aniya. It happened so quickly that the tip of the chair hit Aniya right in the face, just under her eye.

Aniya grabbed the side of her face that hurt, fear written all over her expression. She started to cry hysterically while looking at her mother.

"Get out of my face, now! And I'm not through with you!" her mother yelled.

Aniya quickly ran into her room, crying. Aniya laid across her bed with her head buried deep into her pillow.

"You don't give a damn if a hurricane comes through this place as long as you have that crack pipe to your mouth! It's all good with you!" Anita shouted.

Anita put one hand on her hip while she stared at the man who continued to use the pipe, and ignored her daughter cry from a distance.

"I'm not going to let your brat mess up my high," the man said as he continued to get high while choking at the same time.

"The only one can talk about my child is me, now get the hell out of my house!" she shouted as she knocked everything—including the drugs—off the table.

"Woman, are you crazy? I ought to slap the hell out of you!" the man said as he quickly rose from the table.

Anita grabbed an empty liquor bottle off the cabinet, holding it in the air as if she was about to knock her friend over the head if he tried something. "And if you do it'll be the last face you'll ever slap—now get the hell out my house!"

The man stared at the empty liquor bottle as he took a deep breath. "You're a crazy woman, Nita, crazy I tell you," he said as he headed out the door.

Anita slammed the door behind him. She kicked the mess on her living room floor as she headed to Aniya's room. "You can stop the pouting. It doesn't do anything!" Her hands were on her hips. "Look at me when I'm talking to you!"

Aniya slowly raised her head off her pillow and looked into her mother's eyes with her own swollen and black one.

"Oh God, Niya. I didn't mean, oh God—" Anita said as she rushed over to her daughter, wrapping her arms around her. "Aniya, you know I love you, right? Momma never meant to hurt you, honey. You believe me, don't you?"

"Yes, momma. I'm sorry I upset you," she said as she hugged her mother tightly.

"Oh, you didn't upset me. I guess I was so angry that my only child witnessed her mother in a most shameful act."

Aniya got off the bed as she stared at herself in the mirror. Anita stood behind Aniya. "Mom."

"Don't 'mom' me. If you would have been in the bed like I thought you were instead of sneaking out, this would have never happened," Anita said as she swung Aniya's body to face her.

Aniya put her head down.

"So, don't you think you have some explaining to do Niya? So what was it? Sex or drugs?" she accused while folding her arms.

"What?" Aniya asked, quickly raising her head up as she paused for a second, looking at her mom in shock. "Momma, what are you talking about?" she asked, wiping her tears.

"Aniya, don't take me for a fool. Why would someone be out this time of night? Now answer me. Which one was it? Because job ain't an option."

"Neither! How dare you question me when your life ain't right!"

"Don't raise your voice to me! Besides, this conversation is not about me. Aniya, you are my child. I have the right to question you. You don't pay a damn bill in this house. You can't believe that you can just do what you want to do, and I should have no say so. You may not answer me now, but just so you know, what goes on in the dark comes out into the light."

"Just get out of my room!"

"Just remember what I said!" Anita said as she slammed the door behind her.

Aniya stared at the closed door as she thought about the lie she told her mother.

***

Two weeks had passed, and Malik had come over to Aniya's house. They were sitting on the sofa studying for exams. Malik put away the papers and turned toward Aniya.

"Well, that was a good session ma'am, you should have all As on your exam… or else."

"Or else what?"

"Or else this," Malik said as he kissed Aniya slowly.

"What in the hell is going on here?" Anita hollered as she entered her home. Aniya and Malik jumped apart.

"Hello, Ms. Anita, how are you?" Malik asked as he quickly got up off the sofa, putting his hand out for a handshake.

Anita didn't budge.

"Momma, you remember Malik don't you?" Aniya asked as she rose up off the sofa.

"What did I tell you about having these thugs in my house? Especially when I'm not home?"

"Momma, he's not a thug. He's smart and he is about to graduate."

"Well if he was smart, he would know it's disrespectful to come to my home when I'm not here."

Craig suddenly entered the living room.

Everyone turned to look at him.

Anita turned back, staring at Malik. "I think you better leave, Aniya has housework to do."

"Yes ma'am," Malik said. "I'll see you later," he said as he looked over at Aniya.

"I doubt that very seriously," Anita scowled.

Aniya continued to stare at Craig without saying a word.

Craig put on a grin.

"Later everyone," Malik said as he began walking off.

Craig grabbed him by the shirt. "There will be no later," Craig said, staring into Malik's eyes.

"Let him go!" Aniya shouted.

"Man, get your hands off me!" Malik said.

Craig grinned at Malik, before he let him go.

Malik hurried out.

"From now on, we're going to have new rules in this house," Anita said, staring at Aniya.

"Look, I don't have time for this!" Aniya said as she began walking away.

"Aniya, your mother is talking to you," Craig said deeply.

"So? What do you have to do with this?" Aniya said as she folded her arms.

"Craig will be living with us for a while," Anita stated.

"Why? He has his own place. What does he need to live with us for? You would leave luxury for projects? It just doesn't make sense. Besides, he's a no good man momma."

"My place is too hot right now, so I will be here for a minute—not that it was any of your business. That's not good hospitality you're showing me, young lady."

"So you come to our home to destroy it and put us in danger. What man would do that to a single woman with a child?"

"You better talk to your disrespectful child, Anita."

"Okay, that's enough you two! Now Aniya, go clean that room and do your homework. I know finals are coming up, so get to it!"

***

Night fell and Anita was in her room getting high when Craig opened her bedroom door. "Here baby, some good ole gin and juice over ice, just for you," he said with a smile as he handed over the glass to Anita.

"You're my everything, how will I make this up to you?" Anita said as she waved her hand in the air to the music.

"Oh, don't worry baby, you're already making it up to me," Craig replied, winking at her before exiting the room. He knocked on Aniya's bedroom door, but got no answer.

"Aniya?" However, he didn't get an answer. He slowly peeled open the door and peeked his head in. "Aniya?" he called as he took a step into her room.

After not seeing Aniya, Craig exited her room. He noticed a crack from the broken bathroom door. And as he got closer to the door, he heard Aniya singing in the shower.

"Aniya," he said softly as he peeked through the door.

However, Aniya didn't respond due to her singing. Craig watched Aniya's silhouette from the shower curtains as he licked his lips. He began to step further into the bathroom when Aniya cut off her shower.

"Craig!" Anita shouted.

Craig stopped when he heard his name.

Aniya opened the shower curtain as she reached for her towel. Craig took a deep breath as he closed the bathroom door before Aniya saw him. "Woman, you should be done with all this partying, or whatever you call it! It's getting too late for all this noise!" he shouted in aggravation.

He and Aniya stared at each other while Aniya continued to dry her hair with a towel. Craig's eyes made it up and down Aniya's body, noticing her lace top and lace shorts.

Aniya rolled her eyes at Craig as she quickly entered her room and locked her door behind her. She leaned against the door and took a deep breath.

***

Aniya was in the park writing in her diary as she listened to music with her headphones on. She jumped when she felt someone's hands touch her shoulders. She quickly took off her headset, looking upset as she cut her music off.

"What, are you spying on me now just because you live with us? Doesn't make it right to come spy on me, Craig!"

"It's Mr. Craig to you," he replied, trying to be smart.

Shania and Coretta were walking by when they spotted Aniya from a distance. They began to giggle and point.

"Can you believe someone is paying miss whatever-her-name-is attention?" Coretta said.

"He's an old sugar daddy!" Shania said as Coretta laughed out loud.

"May I see what you have in this diary?" Craig asked.

"No, it's none of your business what I have in my diary," Aniya replied as she closed it.

"Well, we'll see about that!" he said as he snatched her diary up from her hands.

Aniya quickly got up. "Give me my diary back!" she demanded as she reached for it while Craig was turning around, opening her diary.

Coretta and Shania watched them from afar.

"Didn't know the girl had it in her to flirt with older men," Coretta said as she folded her arms and smacked her lips.

"I guess even she can get somebody," Shania replied before she and Coretta burst out laughing.

"Here, I'm just joking around— what's with the attitude girl?" Craig said as he threw Aniya's diary on the ground.

"Let's go, I think my stomach is getting sick from laughing," Coretta said as they walked off together, laughing more.

"Come on, I have a surprise for you," said Craig.

"I don't want to go anywhere with you. Besides, I don't want anything from you. I wish you would just stay out of our lives!" she shouted as she picked her belongings up off of the ground. "Now move out of my way!"

Craig pulled Aniya by the arm. "You have no choice."

"Let me go! You're hurting me!" Aniya called out as Craig pulled her to his car.

Aniya and Craig ended up at the burger shack, sitting at a table by the window. Aniya just stared at her food.

"You're such an ungrateful brat you know," he said as he took a bite of his burger. He dug into his pocket and put a black box on the table.

Aniya just stared at the box without saying a word.

"Well, go ahead. Open it."

"What is it?" Aniya asked, uncaring.

"I guess you'll never know if you don't open it," he stated as he took a sip of his soda.

"What if I don't want to know?"

"Open the damn—" Craig said loudly until he noticed he was in public. He quickly lowered his voice. "Open the box Aniya."

Aniya stared at the box as she slowly grabbed it off the table.

It was at that moment that Malik entered the café.

"Wow, this is beautiful. Is it for my mom?" Aniya asked as she took the silver diamond necklace out of the box.

Malik turned to the sound of Aniya's voice.

"No, it's for you— here let me put it on," Craig said as he got out his seat to put it on Aniya's neck.

"Why would you get this for me?" she asked as he put the necklace on for her.

"I would like to apologize for my behavior. Besides, if I stay with you and your mom for a while, I have to make it a pleasant visit," he said as he turned Aniya's face towards him.

Malik watched from the café bar.

Mommy Help Me

"May I help you?" the cook asked Malik as she pulled a pen from the back of her ear with her notepad in hand. "Excuse me? If you ain't ready to order, move to the side please—you're holding up the line."

Malik turned quickly at the sound of her voice behind the counter. "Um, I'm sorry, a hamburger please," Malik said as he took a seat on the stool next to the counter.

"One hamburger coming up," the waitress said as she popped her gum.

"Come on, let's go. I also have a surprise for your mother," Craig said as he and Aniya got up from the table.

"Whoa, you're just full of surprises today," Aniya said.

Malik turned in the opposite direction as Aniya and Craig passed by him.

Chapter Five

At school, Aniya filtered through her locker when someone covered her eyes.

"Okay, who is this?" Aniya demanded.

"Your prince charming," Malik responded.

"Oh, Ray," Aniya said jokingly.

Malik uncovered her eyes as Aniya turned to face him.

"Ray? Uh…"

"Hi, my prince charming," Aniya said with a gleam in her eye. "What? Why are you staring like that?"

"Nice necklace."

"Oh, thanks, my mom bought it for me."

Malik just played along, but he was trying to figure out why Aniya would lie to him. "Ms. Anita has good taste," he said with a grin.

"I guess she does," Aniya said as she fidgeted with her fingers.

"So, what's up, boo?" Malik asked with a wink towards Aniya.

"You tell me," Aniya said as she played with his shirt.

"Well, I was thinking we could catch a movie or something."

"I don't know Malik, my mom and Craig are going out tonight and I have to study for these finals."

"Now that's a poor excuse. Since when don't I help you study for your finals?"

"I'm sorry, you're right. Besides, I need a break anyway."

"I tell you what, how about we go together to your house and I'll help you study—then off to the movies we go."

"Sounds like a plan," Aniya said with a smile. "Well, I better get to class."

"All right, see you after school," Malik said before he kissed Aniya on the forehead.

***

Malik and Aniya were taking a walk in the park. Enjoying the moonlight and the stars.

"Thanks for the movie, and for helping me study. You're so sweet to me Malik," Aniya said.

"You don't have to thank me, I love studying with you. Plus, I enjoy spending time with you."

"I don't want this to ever end," Aniya said, gazing into Malik's eyes.

"What you mean by that?"

"It's getting closer to that time, Malik, and you're about to graduate and off to college you go—a brand new world for you. It's like my heart is slowly stopping as the time gets closer."

"You say it like it's a bad thing, Aniya. I want to make a better life for myself and for you—for our future."

Malik and Aniya took a seat on a bench inside the park.

"Malik, face it. New surroundings, parties, and not to mention girls—and did I mention girls?"

"You don't have any of that to worry about, Aniya. I told you that already. You have to trust me, just like I have to trust you when I'm going, little lady. There will be parties here, and guys—and did I mention guys?" Malik echoed, trying to be funny as he tickled Aniya's side.

Aniya laughed. "I guess you're right, Malik."

Malik put his arms around Aniya as they looked up at the stars.

Aniya and Malik made it to Aniya's house.

"Well, thank you again for such a lovely evening. I really enjoyed myself," Aniya said.

"It was my pleasure," Malik said before he kissed Aniya.

Craig opened the door, looking at Aniya and Malik with rage. Malik continued kissing Aniya without even noticing him. Craig folded his arms.

"What the hell is going on here?"

Aniya and Malik both jumped at the sound of Craig's voice.

"Craig—" Malik started.

"That's Mr. Craig to you, didn't your momma teach you respect?"

"Hey man, don't talk about my momma."

"What you goin' to do about it?" Craig said as he got up in Malik's face.

"All right, stop it you two!" Aniya shouted as she got between Craig and Malik.

Craig looked down at Aniya as he breathed heavily.

"Get in the house, Aniya. That would be the best thing for you."

"Hey man, you're going to watch how you talk to my girl," Malik growled.

"Your girl? Boy, if you don't remove your ass from my doorway, I'm going to knock the hell out of you," Craig yelled and cracked his knuckles.

"You better do it then," Malik threatened.

"Malik, just leave please," Aniya pleaded as she pushed him away.

"Yeah, Malik, take your girl's advice," Craig said smugly as he stared Malik in the face.

Aniya walked into the house with Craig behind her. Malik watched as Craig turned around, giving him a grin before closing the door in his face. Aniya stormed off to her room. As soon as Aniya closed her bedroom door, Craig stopped it. Aniya turned to face Craig.

"Get out of my room, get away from me, and get out of my life! You make me so sick!" Aniya shouted as she pulled the diamond necklace off of her neck, letting it shatter onto the floor.

"I'm afraid it's not that easy" Craig said as he began taking slow steps toward Aniya.

"Craig, get out of my room! I mean it!"

Craig began to unbuckle his pants, ignoring what Aniya was screaming.

"What are you doing?" Aniya asked as she clutched her body tightly. "Craig…" she said as she backed away slowly.

Aniya screamed.

***

Later on Anita entered her home with two brown grocery bags. Craig walked from out the back, buckling up his pants.

"Hi baby, I didn't know you were here. I'm so glad you are," Anita said as she placed the grocery bags on the kitchen table.

Craig didn't say a word.

Anita began taking the groceries out of the bags, putting things where they belonged.

"Did you get my 6-pack of beer like I asked?" Craig asked as he lit up a cigarette.

"Here you go, baby," said Anita as she pulled the 6-pack out of the grocery bag.

Aniya was unclothed and crying, while picking her clothes up off the floor.

"Where is Aniya?"

"The brat was probably in her room doing Lord knows what," Craig said, brushing Anita off while flicking his cigarette ashes on the floor. "So where were you today? I passed by your girl Shanell—where you said you'd be—but she said she never saw you today."

Anita nervously opened the refrigerator as she put away the eggs.

"Woman, did you hear what I said?" Craig shouted as he hit his hands against the cabinet.

Anita jumped as she placed her hands across her chest.

There was silence as Anita took deep breath.

"I went to sign up for rehab," Anita mumbled.

"Speak up, woman!"

"I said, I went to sign up for a rehab!" Anita shouted back as she slammed the refrigerator and passed Craig, entering into the living room.

"What is this? Some kind of sick joke? I mean, this is the funniest thing that I've ever heard!" Craig laughed hysterically.

"Excuse me?" Anita said as she stared Craig in the face.

"I mean, Nita, you tried that how many times? And failed, time after time."

"Craig, I swear, you can be so cruel at times. But I won't let that get to me. At least not anymore," Anita said as she began fixing her torn up pillows on her couch.

Aniya was in the bathroom, showering and crying. She was scrubbing her body extra hard. She threw the towel and the soap down as she slowly slid down in the tub, letting the shower pour onto her as she continued to cry.

"I don't want to argue about anything I choose to do. This is my house, and I will do as I please."

"Here, take a hit of this, it will make you loosen up a bit. You seem tense for some reason," Craig said as he tried to hand Anita some drugs.

But Anita did not take them.

"You're sad. You know that, right? You're one sad, sick man."

Craig placed the drugs on the table. "We'll see who's really sad," he said. "I'll be back." Then he headed out the door.

Anita took a deep breath as she stared at the drugs placed on the coffee table. "Come on Anita, you can do this. I know you can. You're changing for the better," Anita whispered to herself while pacing back and forth in the living room.

"I know you can, girl, you are such a strong woman," Anita continued to talk to herself. She began pacing back and forth by her table. She then bit her tongue as she stared harder at the drugs.

She couldn't fight the feeling any longer, so she quickly picked up the drugs and used them.

***

"Hurry, we might be losing her!" A nurse shouted as she opened Anita's shirt.

"Momma, momma! Please don't die on me! God, no, I can't lose my momma!" Aniya shouted as she ran down the hospital hall with her mom in the bed, the nurses rushing her into the emergency room.

"Someone get the girl! Get the girl!" a nurse shouted as she tried to hold Aniya back.

"No, please don't let my momma die! Please! I'm begging you! Aniya cried out as she hit the floor. "Oh God no!!"

That was the last thing Aniya cried out.

***

In the waiting room, Aniya was sitting in a chair with her head down. Someone touched Aniya on the back.

"Hey, are you all right?" Malik asked.

Aniya quickly rose from the chair. "Oh, Malik! I'm so glad to see you! Oh God, you don't know how much I've been going through!" Aniya cried as she hugged Malik tightly.

"How is your mom?" Malik asked as he and Aniya took a seat.

"Well, they haven't told me anything yet. I've just been waiting patiently. How did you know I was here?"

"The neighborhood talks," Malik said as he put his head down, fidgeting with his fingers.

"Oh God, more problems. I bet people are saying all kinds of horrible things," Aniya said as she lowered her head.

"Everything will be just fine, I promise. Hold your head up," Malik said as he rubbed Aniya's back.

"Aniya?" A doctor in his white coat stood beside them.

Aniya quickly stood up with Malik by her side. "Yes, doctor? Oh please tell me my mother is okay! Please!" she asked hysterically.

"Your mother is just fine, even though that was a close call. But we're glad you got her in when you did. You're such a brave girl."

Aniya let out a sigh of relief as she placed her hand over her heart.

"However, she came close to overdosing. Next time might not be so good. We'll keep her in overnight for observation, but she must be enrolled in an rehab center."

"May I see her now?" Aniya asked.

"Yes, you may," he said as he walked off.

"Listen, I think you and your mother need some time alone, so I'll go—but I will catch up with you later," Malik said as he held Aniya's hand.

"Yeah, that sounds like a plan."

"Listen, why don't you call me later and we can get together?" Malik suggested.

"I'll try."

Malik kissed Aniya on the forehead, and watched as Aniya walked away. Aniya slowly opened up the hospital room. She saw her mother lying in the bed with her eyes closed and tubes in her nose.

"Oh mommy, you gave me such a scare," she said as she held Anita's hand. "You can't keep doing this, because," Aniya began to cry. "Because you're not only hurting yourself, but you're hurting me so, so bad momma. You're all I have!" She put her head down and cried out loud.

Aniya jumped as she felt someone hug her from behind. She quickly turned around, her sorrow turned into madness.

"Get your arms off me, you creep!"

Craig let go of Aniya. "That's a way to talk to someone when they're trying to comfort you."

"You're a creep, and always will be a creep! I hate you! Don't you ever touch me again! Do you hear me? Don't ever put your dirty hands on me again!"

Anita slowly opened her eyes to the sound of Aniya's voice. "Aniya, was that you?" Anita asked softly.

"Momma," Aniya said as she stood beside her. "I'm so glad you're okay."

"What happened to me?"

Aniya took a deep breath before answering. "Mom, you almost overdosed," she said as she hugged her mother, crying.

Anita looked up at Craig as she rubbed her daughter's head, tears flowing down her cheeks. "I'm sorry you had to witness that, pumpkin. I just keep messing up. Thank God I'm alive."

There's silence.

"I have to change. God, just give me the strength to change! It is you who I need!" Anita cried.

Aniya laid her head on her mother's stomach as Craig put his head down.

***

Night fell as Aniya was in her room putting last minute touches on her hair. There was a knock on the door. Aniya moved from the mirror to open it.

"Wow, you look beautiful," Malik said.

"Thanks," she responded shyly with her head tilted to the side.

"You ready? Or did I come a little too early?"

"No, the sooner we get out of here the better," Aniya joked.

"Shall we?" Malik offered as he reached his hand out to Aniya.

***

In the movie theater, Aniya buried her head in Malik's shirt as a scary part approached.

"And somebody said nothing could scare them. Yeah right! All that big talk for nothing!" Malik said, teasing her.

"Oh, whatever!" Aniya hit him gently.

"Aniya!" someone shouted in the theater.

"It sounds like someone said my name," Aniya said looking around the movie theater.

"Damn, is that movie scary? Oh my God!" Malik said while laughing.

"Aniya!" a man shouted.

"Wait, it really sounds like someone called your name," Malik said as he and Aniya turned around.

Everyone was trying to shut the man up. Aniya and Malik stood as the man got closer.

"Craig!" Aniya shouted. She was in complete shock as her eyes got bigger.

"Young lady, if you know what's good for you, you better leave with me this instant!" Craig shouted, pointing his finger at Aniya.

"Look man, you better get out of the way. I didn't pay to watch your ass!" a guy sitting in the theater said.

"Who you talking to, you little chump? You better shut up before that movie be watching you!" Craig shouted back.

"Craig! Stop it right now. I'm not going anywhere with you, and I mean it!" Aniya said, folding her arms.

"Man, you are really crazy. She said she's going nowhere with you," Malik said, defending her.

"You don't have any wants!" Craig said as he pulled Aniya.

Aniya was pulling away.

"You let her go!" Malik said.

"Or what?"

"Look man, I don't want beef with you. I'll take her home," Malik said as he put up his hand.

"Get out the way!" Some of the people started to shout as they threw popcorn at Aniya, Malik, and Craig. Craig snatched Aniya by the arm.

"Bring your ass on home before I get crazy," Craig said, looking like he was ready to kill.

Craig held Aniya's arm as they walked up the aisle.

"I said, let her go!" Malik cried as he began walking up to Craig.

"I'm going to have to teach you some manners!" Craig snapped as he let Aniya go, walked up to Malik, and punched him in the face.

Malik and Craig got into a tumble while Aniya was screaming for them to stop. Security came to break them up and escorted them out of the theater.

Malik was wiping the blood from his nose as Aniya tried to comfort him.

"Aniya," Craig said as he wiped blood off of his lip.

Aniya looked furiously at Craig.

"I'll be waiting for you at home," Craig said. Aniya made an angry face as she turned back to Malik.

"Are you okay?" Aniya asked while rubbing his face.

"Yeah, I'll be okay."

"Come on, let's go," Aniya said as she and Malik held hands to the car.

Malik opened the door as Aniya got in. "I'm sorry, I'm so sorry I ruined the night. I didn't expect this to happen," Aniya said as she put her hand on top of Malik's.

"It's not your fault, Aniya," Malik leaned over and kissed Aniya on the lips. Aniya smiled as Malik started the car and took off.

"Something has to be done about that man, Aniya," Malik said as he pulled in front of Aniya's apartment. "I just wish there was something I could do."

"I know, me too! God, I hate that man so much. You don't know how much I hate him!" Aniya said as she put her head down.

Malik passed his fingers through her hair. "You know, I don't think you should be home alone with this man. It's like he's obsessed with you or something."

"Me neither, he really scares me. And you know what?"

"What?"

"Uh… nothing," Aniya said, getting nervous that she'd let the wrong thing out.

Craig watched Aniya and Malik through the broken blinds in the apartment.

"You know, tonight I really want to go to the hospital and be with my mom since they kept her longer than expected."

"I think that's a great idea. I think something really bad will happen if you stay here, Aniya," Malik said as he pulled off.

Craig stepped outside as he watched the car drive away.

"All right Malik, you continue to push my buttons and I will have to do away with you," Craig said to himself as he stood outside the apartment watching the car leave the area.

***

At the hospital, Aniya and Malik entered Anita's room.

"Momma," Aniya said as she stood by her mother side.

Anita looked at her daughter and stared for a moment. "Oh, I'm so sorry Aniya. I know you've heard me say that a million times."

Anita sighed, "I hate putting you through this. I keep thinking that I will quit, but I keep messing up."

"You can sign up for rehab. Maybe that will help this time because you are willing to change."

"Yeah, then child protection services will come and get you. You know I can't leave you like that. No telling how long they will keep me in rehab. You're my baby no matter what Aniya, no matter how much we bicker; I love you with all my heart. You hear me child?"

"Yes ma'am. I love you so much momma, you're all I have."

"What are you doing out this time of the night anyway?" Anita questioned.

"Well, Malik and I went out for a movie, then we decided to come here."

"Hello," Malik said from the doorway.

"Malik, you mean to tell me you been in here and didn't say a word? Come here so I can see you."

Malik walked to Anita and stood beside her. "I know how much you disagree with me being with your daughter. I really don't want to upset you, especially at a time like this," he said while scratching the top of his head. "I hope you get better soon."

"Don't worry, I'll be all right," Anita said as she smiled at Malik.

It got quiet.

"You really love my daughter, don't you Malik?"

Malik smiled as he looked at Aniya.

"Mom—"

"I do love her," Malik responded.

Aniya blushed.

"Now, you better not break my baby's heart. I will come after you," Anita joked. "You treat my daughter well and provide things I can't provide. You really stick by her side throughout school as well."

"I promise I won't break her heart, and that's what boyfriends are for."

Aniya smiled at Malik as she thought to herself, "He better not break that promise, or else."

"Well, I guess I better get going and let you two be alone," Malik said as he took his hands off the rail of the bed.

"Why don't you stay a while, help me to get to know you better?" Anita said with a smile.

Malik and Aniya just smiled at each other.

Chapter Six

As time went by, Aniya began to get sick. She couldn't figure out what was causing it. Day after day she was sleepy and nauseous. It was beginning to take a great toll on her.

In class, the students were rowdy because there was no teacher around yet. They were chatting away about an upcoming football game, girls being messy, or anything else they could think of. It was always something.

Malik and Aniya were chatting as the captain of the cheerleading squad stepped in the room. Everyone stopped talking and gave her their undivided attention—except Aniya. Everyone respected her because of her popularity.

Aniya kept talking to Malik.

"I mean, like, really, who was she supposed to be?" Aniya said as she swung her hair to one side.

"So, are you coming by my house today?" Malik asked Aniya.

"Hi, Malik," the cheer captain, Christina, said suggestively. She was in her cheerleading outfit with a fitted top and short skirt. She took her seat across from Malik, licking her lollipop.

"Hi there, Christina," Malik said, as if Aniya wasn't there.

"So, are you coming to my party Friday night?" she asked as she crossed her legs, holding up her lollipop.

"Yeah sure, we would love to come," Malik responded as he bit his lip.

"Come again? Who is the 'Oui'?" Christina said with a fake French accent.

"Me and my girl Aniya," Malik said while smiling at Christina.

"I'm sorry? Did you hear me inviting Aniya? Because maybe I might have missed that," Christina said with attitude, staring at her lollipop.

Malik's smile disappeared from his face.

"That's all right Malik. Being around a bunch of snobs doesn't excite me—you go. I have better things to do with my time anyway," Aniya said as she folded her legs while opening a book.

"Okay class, let's open your books to chapter five," the teacher, Mrs. Patricia, announced as she walked in the room.

Aniya raised her hand.

"What is it, Aniya?" Mrs. Patricia said as she slid her glasses down her nose impatiently.

"May I be excused to the restroom?" Aniya asked, holding her stomach.

"You had time to go before class, so the answer is no. I don't understand you children—the older you get, the worse it is."

"Mrs. Patricia, I really need to go. It's an emergency."

"Aniya, my final answer was no, now that's the end of this discussion—and please don't interrupt me again," Mrs. Patricia said as she began to write on the board.

"Whatever, I shouldn't have asked you anyway," Aniya said as she rose from her chair and proceeded to leave the classroom.

"Aniya! Aniya!" Mrs. Patricia shouted as the rest of the class watched in silence.

"Aniya, baby!" Malik called.

"I'm going to write her up. She is going to do what she wants anyway," Mrs. Patricia said as she grabbed a pen and paper.

"What's wrong with her having to go to the restroom?" Malik exclaimed.

"Malik—not now. I'm not about to participate in a conversation with you about your girlfriend."

Aniya vomited in the hallway.

Malik ran out the classroom and into the hall where he spotted Aniya bent over, holding her stomach. "Aniya, are you okay?" Malik asked as he rubbed Aniya's back.

"I don't know," Aniya admitted as she slowly rose up, wiping her mouth with her sleeve.

Christina stopped by Malik and Aniya on the way to the office, with a paper in her hand as she shook her head in disgust. "Malik, I would have never thought you would lower your standards and give somebody like this a chance," she said as she walked off.

Aniya just stared at Malik and backed away from him. "You're going to let her talk to me like that and not respond back?" she said as she walked away and into the restroom.

Malik looked as if today was the end of the world as he took a deep breath.

***

Later that day, Aniya was in her bedroom, lying down across her bed when her mother entered.

"Aniya, take this food stamp card and go to the store to buy some ham and bread, we don't have anything in this house to eat."

"Momma, I can't. I don't feel good."

"What's wrong with you?"

"I don't know, I keep vomiting and I can't keep anything down."

"Well, it must be some type of virus going around. I'll just go to the store myself and bring you back some soup."

"Thanks ma, I really appreciate it."

Aniya then fell asleep on her stomach.

Minutes later, her door slowly opened.

Craig entered Aniya's room as he stood on the side of her bed with a grin. He rubbed Aniya from her back to her buttocks.

Until she began to stir.

As soon as her eyes opened, Craig yanked her hair back.

Aniya let out a loud screech. "Let my hair go, Craig!!"

"Shut up! Now this will be painful if you don't cooperate!" Craig said furiously.

"No please, don't, please!" Aniya cried as she tried to break free from Craig.

Just then, there was a knock on the door.

Aniya turned around quickly as Craig's concentration broke. She kicked him in his groin. Craig hit the floor as Aniya immediately took off, running out of the room.

Aniya quickly opened the door and ran into Malik's arms.

"Malik, thank God you're here!" Aniya said, breathing heavily.

"Whoa! Whoa! I never thought you were this happy to see me!"

"Let's go! I don't care where we go, just as long as we leave! Please."

"Ok, ok, whatever you want! Is everything okay?"

***

At the coffee shop, Malik was sitting at the coffee table alone until Aniya took a seat next to him. She stared at the table without saying a word.

"Baby, are you all right? You've been sick for quite some time now."

Aniya held her stomach as she laid her head on her hand. "I'll be fine. I'm sure it's just a virus or something."

"But baby, don't you think it's lasting a little too long? I think you should go to the doctor to check yourself. Besides, you don't look so well," he said as he took a sip of his frappe.

"I will," she said weakly while rubbing her head.

She smiled at Malik.

"Why are you smiling at me like that?" Malik said with a grin.

"I love you so much. You always come to my rescue, whether you realize it or not."

Malik winked.

***

One sunny day, Aniya was taking a walk when she noticed a couple moving into a home near the apartments she lived in.

Aniya began to rub her stomach, before she vomited all over the sidewalk. She began to break a sweat.

The lady that was moving in put her box down as she tapped her husband.

"Yes, honey? What is it?" her husband asked.

The woman continued to stare at Aniya while pointing. "Look, there's a girl vomiting. I think she needs help."

"Let's go see about her," he said.

The lady and the man both walked over to Aniya. "Honey, are you all right?" she asked as she rubbed Aniya on the back.

"I think so," Aniya said as she slowly raised her head up, keeping her hand on her stomach.

"Do you need a glass of water?" he asked.

"No, I'll be fine."

"By the way, my name is Nancy. This is my husband, Jeff."

Aniya shook hands with the couple. "Nice to meet you both. I'm sorry it had to be this way."

"Yeah, it's okay. We're just moving into the neighborhood," Nancy said.

"Good luck. This neighborhood gets pretty rowdy and out of control at times," Aniya said.

"I'm assuming you live somewhere around here?" Nancy asked.

"Yes, the projects across the streets. I'm sure you can handle it." Aniya said.

It got quiet for a second.

"Well, I better get home. I'm not feeling too well," Aniya concluded. She rubbed her stomach up and down.

"Of course," Jeff said.

"Maybe we'll see you around," Nancy added.

"I'm sure we will. I just hope I'm in a better situation," Aniya said tiredly before letting out a great big yawn.

Aniya made it home and greeted her mom in the front room.

"Where have you been? I've been calling your phone. You give me a hassle when I don't put minutes on your phone, but when I call you don't answer. I don't put minutes on your phone just so you can talk to, what's his name?" Anita lectured.

"His name is Malik. Momma, I have been throwing up on the way here, so I couldn't talk to anyone!"

"You seem to always take up for this boy, and lately you act like he is your world—like you have nothing else to focus on, child."

"Mom, he's going to college soon. We only have a month left of school and I don't know when I'll see him again."

"It seems like it's more than that. Did you have sex with this Malik?"

Craig walked into the living room. Aniya looked up at him and froze.

"Child, did you hear what I just asked you?" Anita asked as she rose from the sofa.

"Go ahead, answer your mother," Craig said with a grin upon his face.

Aniya looked back at her mother, "No, momma. I didn't."

"Well, we'll see about that. I will make you a doctor's appointment."

"What?" Aniya blinked. She couldn't believe her mother wouldn't take her word. "Why would you do that?"

"Well, if you have nothing to hide it shouldn't be a problem," Anita replied as she stared Aniya in the eyes.

Aniya stormed off into her room.

***

At the doctor's office, the nurse walked into the room that Aniya and her mother were waiting in.

"Okay Aniya, we will get urine from you and then take it from there. Okay, honey?" the nurse said as she handed Aniya the urine cup.

"Okay, fine," Aniya said, accepting the cup.

The nurse exited the room.

Aniya got off the bed in her hospital robe when her mother grabbed both of her arms gently.

"Aniya, you have one more chance to let me know if you've been having intercourse with this boy Malik," Anita warned as she placed her hand under Aniya's chin.

"Momma," Aniya began as a tear rolled down her face.

"Oh God," Anita said as she placed her hand on her heart.

The nurse came into the room.

"Aniya, you're pregnant," Anita said with total shock.

Aniya burst out crying.

"Dammit, I can barely take care of you!" Anita punched the wall.

Aniya's tears continued to flow as she entered the restroom with her body against the door, holding her cup.

***

School was over and Aniya was at her locker. As Aniya closed her locker, she jumped. Her textbook hit the floor.

"Malik! You scared me!" she said, placing her hand over her heart.

"I'm sorry," he said while picking up her book. "Where are you headed?"

"Home," Aniya said, brushing Malik off.

"Look," he said while grabbing Aniya's arm so that she faced him. "I don't know what's going on with you lately, but we only have two more weeks before I graduate. And for someone who's supposed to love me so much, you're giving me the cold shoulder and acting pretty strange with me, Aniya."

"Really? I haven't noticed. I'm sorry," she responded as she burst into tears.

"Aniya, what is bothering you? You can tell me anything, I love you Aniya," he said as he placed his hand under her chin to raise up her head.

"Your life is just beginning, and mine is just ending," she cried as she buried her face in his chest.

"Aniya, what do you mean by that?" Malik asked. "Are we going to get into it about me going to college for the thousandth time?"

Aniya took a deep breath. "Malik, there's something you should know. I can't keep this from you any longer."

"Malik, you ready for some practicing at my house?" one of his football team members asked while passing by Malik and Aniya.

"I'll meet ya'll later man, I'm with my girl right now."

"That's cool dog, holla at me later."

"Fa sho."

***

Malik was walking Aniya home. "So, what's on your mind?" Malik asked as he held Aniya's hand tighter.

"Well," Aniya said as she took a deep breath. "You know that lately I've been sick and vomiting over everything in sight."

"Yea, and you don't want to go to the doctor."

"Well, I went," Aniya said as she and Malik stopped walking. Aniya faced Malik.

"Okay, what'd they say?"

"Malik, I'm pregnant."

There was silence.

"Malik, did you hear what I said? I'm pregnant."

"Yea, yea," Malik said as if he just came back to reality. "Wow." He let Aniya's hand go, turning away from her with his hand on his head.

"Well Malik, say something."

"This is the first time I'm lost for words," he said as he placed his hands on his head. "Does your mom know?"

"She's the one who took me to the doctor, Malik."

Malik took a deep breath. "Oh boy, what did she say?"

"She was furious, Malik, what do you think? I'm only sixteen years old." Malik watched Aniya in silence. "Besides, she said she's telling your momma. She thinks your mom should know."

"What?"

Aniya just put her head down. "What's wrong? What do you have to hide, Malik?"

"Are you serious right now, Aniya? My mom would go crazy! She already doesn't want me with you. I'm about to go to college and you're going to ask me what I have to hide?"

"You act like this news is only going to tear your world apart. What do you think this does to me?" Aniya shouted back, tears rolling down her face. "Dammit! My life will be changed forever! At least you're finishing school! I've got a good ways to go, plus raising a child. I can't stand here and argue with you! I'll walk myself home! I don't need you or anybody else!" she yelled as she stormed off.

"Aniya!" Malik called as he noticed an old couple across the street watching him, shaking their heads.

"What are ya'll looking at, huh?" Malik shouted with his hands in the air.

***

Aniya was in her room on the floor, clutching her pillow tight while crying her eyes out.

Malik was at home in his room, sitting at his desk trying to do his homework when he let out a scream, turning over his desk. He then punched a hole in the wall.

Sandra opened his bedroom door quickly as she spotted Malik with his hands on his head, pacing back and forth in the room.

"Hey boy, what's your problem?" she asked as her eyes became huge with notice to a hole in the wall. "And by the way, you don't pay anything here to be making holes you can't fix!" She put her hands on her hips. "What's going on? Why are you flipping furniture in my house, boy?"

Malik was still pacing, ignoring his mother. "Malik, what is the problem?"

"Momma, you would never understand," he said as he flopped in his chair.

"How could I understand if you don't tell me what the problem is?" Sandra said as she took a deep breath. "Is it dealing with school, Malik?"

"No ma'am."

"Is it football?"

"No, mom," Malik responded angrily.

"If it's about that little tramp of a girl you call a girlfriend, I don't want to hear it!"

"Mom, how could you say something like that?" he said, standing up. "You don't even know her, but you're judging her. What kind of message are you sending to your kids, thinking we're better than everybody? We wouldn't have anything either if a daddy I never met wouldn't send child support!"

Suddenly, a hand hit his face.

"How dare you talk to your mother like that for a piece of trash!" she said, staring him in the eyes as Malik held the side of his face. "I will not allow that talk in my house! I've been too good to your sister and you, doing the best I could so you could have everything, and this is the thanks I get?"

"I'm just tired of you talking trash about someone I love! I mean how do you think that makes me feel?"

"I think I've heard enough!" she said as she exited the room and slammed his door behind her.

***

Aniya was taking a stroll in her neighborhood. But as she turned the corner, she bumped into Nancy on the sidewalk.

"Oh my God!" Nancy said as she quickly took off her headphones. She noticed Aniya holding her stomach. "Are you okay?"

"Yeah I'm fine," Aniya responded softly as she took her hand off her stomach. "Nice outfit," she added as she looked up at Nancy.

"Oh thanks, this is my exercising outfit. Got to keep it stylish while keeping fit!" Nancy jokingly replied as she did a quick pose.

"There's nothing wrong with that!" Aniya said as she and Nancy laughed.

It got quiet.

"So where were you headed?" Nancy asked.

"Just taking a walk to clear my mind."

"Cool, is it okay if I join you?"

"Suit yourself. Don't know if I would be great company at this particular time."

"Well, let me be the judge of that." Nancy replied as they continued to walk.

"So, care to share what's going on? Maybe I can be a help to you."

"No, that's okay. It looks like the more people I tell, the more problems that come with it."

"I promise I won't become a problem. Maybe I can help you!"

Aniya looked up at Nancy. "I promise," Nancy said with her hand in the air as if she was swearing.

"Well, I have this friend," Aniya started hesitantly.

"Okay, go on."

"Well, she and this guy are dating. They've been dating for a while, and she wound up pregnant. But she doesn't think the guy is too happy about it."

"Why doesn't she think the guy was happy about it?"

"First off, this girl is in the 10th grade, and he graduates from high school in another week and begins his new life at college."

"Wow, so this guy is pretty young."

"Yes," Aniya mumbled as she put her head down.

"And how old is the girl, if you don't mind me asking?"

"She's 16," Aniya replied as she and Nancy stop walking. Aniya looked Nancy in the face.

"You know, I deal with cases like this all the time."

"Really?"

"Of course. I'm a motivational speaker. I motivate high school students all over the world. I will be speaking at Mackelyn High."

"Wow, that's where I go to school."

Aniya and Nancy made it to the front of Nancy's house.

"Well Aniya, I'm sorry to hear this news about your friend. If you think she would like someone to talk to, I would be glad to help."

"Sure, I'll let her know," Aniya replied softly as she looked down at the ground.

Nancy gave Aniya a stare. "Would you like to come in my home for a second?"

"Well," Aniya said hesitantly as she took a look back at her apartment complex.

"Oh come on, only for a second?"

"Why not," Aniya said as she shrugged her shoulders. "I haven't got a life anyway."

***

Nancy and Aniya were laughing over tea.

"May I please use your restroom?" Aniya asked as she placed her tea on the coffee table.

"Sure, down the hall to your left."

"Thank you."

As Aniya came out from the restroom she heard a noise from a nearby room. She looked cautiously down the hall before creeping into a half opened door. She spotted a room that seemed to be nursery. There were baby items thrown all around the room.

Aniya was confused when she saw a broken down baby crib in the corner covered with a pink blanket. There was a pink diaper hamper and a lot of pink stuffed animals lying on the floor. Baby music was playing from a little toy radio in the corner of the room.

Aniya took a closer look at the rug, and whispered the name written on it. "Zhori."

"Aniya, what are you doing in my room?"

Aniya jumped. "I was just—"

"You 'were just' nothing," Nancy said as she pulled Aniya out of the room. Nancy slammed the door behind her.

"I'm sorry, okay?" Aniya said, though she didn't see what the problem was.

Nancy took a deep breath. "Please forgive me, I'm really sorry. I didn't mean to snap at you," Nancy said as she held her head with both of her hands.

"I didn't know you were a mother."

"I'm not."

"Well, what's all the baby stuff for?"

"That is none of your business. What's in my room is none of your concern!"

Aniya and Nancy just stared at one another.

Just then, Jeff entered the hallway. "Well, hello, ladies," he said excitedly. But he then noticed the tension between Nancy and Aniya. "Is everything all right?"

"Everything is just fine," Nancy said with a forced smile.

"Yeah, I was just leaving."

"See you around at school," Nancy said, still holding her fake smile.

"Yea, whatever."

***

At school, Malik was sitting with his teammates enjoying his lunch. Aniya was sitting with one of her friends. Every now and then Aniya and Malik looked up at each other before quickly looking away.

"Hey girl! What's up with you and Malik lately?" Ja'nariah, Aniya's friend, asked her as she took a sip of her soda.

"Malik? I don't know who you're talking about."

"Well you sure could've fooled me, cause you can't keep your eyes off of him and he can't keep his eyes off of you."

"Girl, I want to tell you, but I can't."

"Look," Ja'nariah said as she pointed in the opposite direction of where Aniya was looking.

Aniya turned quickly.

"Aniya, can we talk?" Malik asked as he gazed into Aniya's eyes.

"Sure, go ahead," Aniya said, annoyed at his sudden approach.

"I mean in private."

"Listen girl, we will catch up later," Ja'nariah said before disappearing.

***

Aniya and Malik were walking down the hall while other students were at their lockers, chatting with friends. Some were bopping and talking on cellphones.

"So, how're you feeling?" Malik asked.

"Oh, you concerned all of a sudden?" Aniya asked sassily as she twirled her hair with her finger.

"Yes, I am concerned Aniya. Otherwise I wouldn't be asking you anything," Malik said as he and Aniya stopped by her locker.

Meanwhile, Mrs. Landry was walking Nancy around the school so she could be familiar with her environment. "So, as you can see, some of our kids are more active than others—but you'll soon come to know that each child that comes here comes from different environments. Well, we are to the end of our tour, any questions?"

"No thanks, it looks like I've got it from here," Nancy said with great confidence.

"Okay, see you tomorrow."

"Can't wait to start."

"You giving me the cold shoulder won't help anything, Malik. One minute you act concerned and another minute you're acting like this was all my fault and make me feel guilty.

"So excuse me if I don't know how to respond to all of your different emotions," Aniya said as she began to put in the combination of her locker.

"Dammit, Aniya!" Malik said as he hit the locker, just missing Aniya's face. Aniya jumped without saying a word.

"All this animosity between us won't solve anything! You're carrying!" He noticed that other classmates were staring in their direction. "You are carrying my child, Aniya. We need to figure out what we are going to do from this point on."

Nancy noticed Malik and Aniya and began to walk in their direction. Shania walked behind Nancy when she noticed her watching Malik and Aniya.

"Yes, I'm carrying your child that you don't believe is yours! There, I said it. Are you happy?"

Nancy covered her mouth in shock and stopped dead in her tracks with her eyes glued on Malik and Aniya. "You've got to be kidding me!" Shania said as she placed her hand on her hip. Nancy quickly turned around at the sound of Shania's voice.

Malik grabbed his head in frustration. Nancy continued to stare at Shania.

"Excuse me, do you know them?" Nancy asked.

"I don't know much about Miss. Pocahontas but I do know about the handsome prince over there." Some kids whispered about what they just heard and some watched Aniya walk away. Malik fell back against the locker in frustration and humiliation.

"Malik hi! Are you okay?" Shania asked as she placed her hand on his chest.

"I'm sorry, Shania. I'm in no mood to talk," said Malik as he walk away.

The bell rang and the kids moved along to their classrooms. Aniya was in the restroom, throwing up horribly. Nancy walked into the bathroom. After quickly hearing the horrible retching sound, Nancy knocked on the restroom stall.

"Are you okay in there?"

Nancy got no reply as the girl continued to vomit. "Hey, are you okay?" she asked again as she placed her ear to the stall.

Aniya got off the floor as she wiped her mouth. "Honey, I can help you if you let me," Nancy said gently.

Aniya flushed the toilet, and then unlocked the bathroom stall. She opened the door and looked up at Nancy. She passed by her without saying a word.

"Aniya," Nancy said as her eyes followed Aniya to the sink.

Aniya turned on the water to rinse her hands and her mouth.

"Aniya, honey, are you okay?"

"So you started today, huh?" Aniya asked, changing the subject immediately.

"Yes I did, but are you okay?"

"I'm just fine," Aniya said as she turned off the water and grabbed a paper towel.

"Well, if you need anything I'll be here."

"I won't need anything from you," Aniya said before she threw the paper towel in the trash and walked out of the restroom.

Nancy took a deep breath as she folded her arms.

Chapter Seven

Aniya was walking on the sidewalk to her apartment.

As Aniya got closer to her home, she spotted Craig standing on the steps with his arms folded. Aniya began breathing faster as she got closer. She walked up the steps without saying a word to him, but Craig quickly snatched her arm.

Next door, Nancy pulled into her driveway.

"So, are we not going to speak?"

Aniya continued to breathe fast without saying a word.

"I see Anita isn't doing a good job raising you. You still don't have manners."

Nancy was walking to her mailbox when she saw what was happening next door.

"Get your hands off of me, you creep! Why haven't you left yet? I get sick every time I look at your face!" she said, pulling away from Craig.

Nancy was stunned at what she saw.

"Go right ahead, you won't amount to anything. You'll be just like your mother, you pregnant wench!" Craig said as he let go, letting Aniya fall back against the front door.

Nancy took off in Craig's direction when someone honked the horn at her. Nancy turned around quickly.

"Where you going, sexy lady?" her husband asked teasingly while waving one hand out the window.

Mommy Help Me

"Something is happening across the street. I was going to check it out."

"What's going on across the street?" Jeff questioned as he stepped out of the car.

Nancy turned around and noticed that Aniya was no longer outside. Craig however, was now staring at her.

"Nancy?" Jeff asked, confused.

"I guess it was nothing," she said hesitantly as she turned back to Jeff.

Jeff and Nancy walked into their house. Jeff placed his bag on the kitchen table and accepted a glass of wine from his wife.

"Wine, food... all smelling good!" Jeff exclaimed while lifting the pot's lid.

"Uh-uh," Nancy said as she quickly placed the lid on top of the pot, smiling at her husband. "It's a surprise."

"It's not our anniversary, nor any of our birthdays," Jeff said as he leaned against the kitchen cabinets.

"That's where you're wrong," Nancy said while walking over to the kitchen table.

Jeff looked confused and raised his eyebrow at her. To answer, Nancy pulled the lid off of the container in the middle of the table.

"Ta-dah!"

Jeff stared at the cake she revealed. There was a large number one in the middle of it. "Nancy, what are you doing?" he asked angrily as he raised an eyebrow at Nancy.

"It's our daughter's first birthday, Jeff!"

"Woman, are you crazy?"

"What?" she asked as the smile started to leave her face.

"We have no daughter Nancy."

"What?" Nancy gasped as she slammed the lid against the table. "What do you mean we have no daughter? I gave birth to your child, Jeff! How could you say such a thing? Did you forget about her already? Did you forget about your only child?" she screamed, tears rolling down her face.

"Nancy, she's gone! She will never come back! Listen, you have to stop doing this! It's enough that we lost her, but now you're planning parties?"

"Lately she's been in my dreams more that she's ever been. Like she's reminding me of how big she's becoming," said Nancy as a tear rolled down her cheek.

Jeff placed his glass of champagne on the table as he took his glasses off, wiping tears from his eyes. "Nancy, this was insane—you have to pull yourself together. Our child is in heaven, baby."

Nancy stared at Jeff in disbelief.

***

"Listen, I'm going to go shower. I can't take any more of this," Jeff said as he walked out of the kitchen.

"Damn!" Nancy shouted as she threw her glass of champagne against the wall. She fell to the floor in tears.

***

It was midnight when Jeff slowly opened his eyes. He realized that Nancy was no longer beside him. He slipped on his slippers and rose from bed. He walked into the kitchen, spotting Nancy at the table with her back to him. She was staring at the cake.

Jeff lowered his head.

"Nancy, honey," he started.

She didn't reply.

"Listen Nancy, I didn't mean to get upset earlier," he said, walking up to her and massaging her shoulders. "I love her as much as you. Trust me I do. I hurt just as much as you—but honey, you have to let her rest in peace." He kissed the top of her head.

"Oh, Jeff!" Nancy cried as she rose from her chair to hug Jeff tightly.

"We're going to be just fine, you know. I believe she's in Heaven, watching down on us each and every day. Besides, she's even closer to us than we think because we keep her so close in our hearts."

***

On Graduation Day, the graduating class threw up their caps in celebration. Everyone was screaming for the students. Malik hugged his mother as his sister and Shania stood beside him. Aniya watched from afar.

"Hey, aren't you going to congratulate your man?" a voice asked from behind her.

Aniya turned around to find Malik's best friend Ron standing there.

"Hi Ron, congrats," she said as she hugged him.

"Thanks! It's been a hard road, but I made it."

"You sure did. I'm proud of you, Ron."

"So, aren't you going to give my boy his props?"

Aniya looked in Malik's direction when she witnessed him and Shania hugging. Aniya took a deep breath before saying, "Well, I was just going to wait for the right moment." She lowered her head.

"Well, no time like the present," Ron said.

"I know you're right," Aniya said, giving him another hug.

"As soon as we have our diplomas you put your hands all over my girl," Malik joked as he walked up to the pair.

Ron and Aniya stopped hugging and smiled as Malik approached them.

Ron and Malik hugged as Ron shouted, "We did it man!"

"Of course! There was no doubt we would, man!"

"Well, I better go see my family!" Ron said, giving Malik a handshake. Ron took off running, cheering with excitement with his graduation cap up in one hand.

"Well? Are you just going to stand there?" Malik asked Aniya with his arms open.

She hugged him tight. "It might not seem like it, but I'm very proud of you Malik. I want your new beginning to be filled with happiness. I love you so much," said Aniya as she squeezed Malik tighter.

"It will be, because I'll have you in it," Malik said. He kissed her lips as he held her tightly.

Sandra, along with his grandmother, walked up to him and Aniya.

"I hope this summer goes fast so this foolishness can stop," Sandra said.

Malik and Aniya immediately pulled apart from one another.

"And who is this lovely young girl?" Malik's grandmother, asked.

"This is Aniya. Aniya, this is my grandma, Silva," Malik said.

"What a pleasure to meet such a pretty young lady," Silva said as she reached her arms out to Aniya for a hug.

Aniya looked at Malik. She didn't want to make the wrong move with his family.

"In this family, we believe in hugging," Silva said jokingly.

Aniya smiled and hugged Silva.

Sandra was glancing around when she noticed Craig standing on the fringe of the crowd. He was in his black suit and was putting a cigar in his mouth. She quickly turned her head back to Malik, breaking eye contact with Craig.

"Won't you all excuse me? I believe I forgot something," said Sandra as she picked up her purse and put it over her shoulder.

***

Craig watched the scene for a minute, and then proceeded to leave.

"What are you doing here?" inquired Sandra. "I don't remember sending you a memo.""

Craig took out a cigar as he grinned.

"Really, Sandra. I didn't know you were still into playing games," said Craig as he lit his cigar. "As long as you have something that belongs to me, I will forever be invited. May I add you look as good as the first time I laid eyes on you."

"Look, I don't have time for this nonsense. Just stay away from me and my family. You got that?" demanded Sandra as she began to walk away.

"Sandra, now you know I can't do that. I think I just might be seeing a little more of you guys that usual," said Craig as he puffed on his Cigar.

Sandra stopped right where she was, walking but never turned to look at Craig as she breathed heavily.

***

"Bitch, I know it was you!" said Craig as Anita's body hit the lamp as she fell to the floor.

"I swear! I swear! I didn't steal from you, Craig!" Anita shouted. "Help me, please!" she called out as she kicked Craig off of her.

Anita was squirming away when Craig grabbed her hair, yanking her head back. Anita screamed in pain.

Aniya woke up at the sound of her mother's screams. "Momma!" she yelled as she jumped out of bed.

"Your ass better come up with my drugs before I kill you!" Craig said. He raised his fist, ready to punch Anita where she lay.

"Leave my momma alone!" Aniya shouted as she quickly picked up the discarded lamp. She raised it as high as she could and hit Craig in the head.

"Tramp!" Craig yelled as he started breathing heavily. Aniya backed up slowly.

"Run!" Anita shouted suddenly.

Aniya screamed for help as she ran for the door. She opened it, but Craig was faster and slammed it shut with one hand.

"Leave my child alone!" Anita shouted as she rose up from the floor.

Craig grabbed Aniya by the neck. "Child, you should know better than to get mixed up in adult business."

"Let go of me!" Aniya said, her voice strained as tears started to fall down her face.

Anita looked in the corner and noticed a wooden bat. "You don't have anything to do with what's going on, little girl," Craig snarled, staring at Aniya with anger in his eyes.

"Let her go!" Anita shouted as she wacked Craig in the back of the head. Craig stumbled and let Aniya go.

Aniya quickly opened the door and ran out.

"Come back here, girl!" Craig shouted after her.

Aniya was crossing the street as she looked back at her house. A car honked loudly at her and it's brakes squealed as it stopped right in front of her. Aniya put one hand over her heart.

"Hey, stay out the way! Next time you might not be so lucky!" said an old white man, his hand swinging out of the car at her, swatting her away.

Aniya ignored him and continued across the street until she reached another house. She banged on her neighbor's door.

Jeff opened the door.

"Oh, help us! Please!" Aniya cried.

"Honey, what's wrong?" Nancy said as she ran into the living room, putting on her robe.

"Please hurry, he's going to hurt my mother!" Aniya pleaded.

"Honey, call the cops!" Jeff said before taking off running across the street.

"Come in here, honey," Nancy said as she reached her hand out to Aniya.

Tears flowed down Aniya's cheeks as she watched Jeff run towards her home.

"Come on, I'm calling the police. Everything will be all right, I promise."

***

Later that night, Jeff and Nancy heard a knock on their door.

"Who is it?" Nancy asked as she put on her robe.

"You know who it is. Now open this door and let my child out right this minute," Anita yelled.

Nancy swung the door open and said, "Can you please keep it down before you wake up the neighbors?"

"I don't give a damn about the neighbors," Anita said, glaring menacingly at Nancy.

"Look, why don't you just let her rest here for the night. It's already late."

"That's what she's got a house for. She can rest at her own damn house!"

"It's okay, I'll go home," Aniya said as she walked up behind Nancy, her arms were folded across her chest.

Nancy wrapped her arm around Aniya and asked her, "Are you okay?"

"I'm fine. I'll see you tomorrow, okay?" Aniya shook her head as she made her way to the door.

Anita and Aniya walked off as Aniya took a look back at her neighbor's home. Nancy stood in the doorway and blew a kiss to Aniya. Aniya gave her a gentle smile as she walked off. As Aniya and Anita walked to their apartment, Anita spoke up.

"You know, there is something about that Nancy that I don't like. I can't put my finger on it, but time will soon reveal it."

"Mom, would you stop?" Aniya pleaded as she stopped in place.

Anita stopped walking as well.

"Aniya, this is not up for discussion," she said.

"Nothing is ever up for discussion with you. You don't know her, but you're judging her already!"

"Shut up, just shut up! I have a bad feeling about her and when I get a feeling like that, I'm always right."

Nancy watched the two women argue from her window.

Anita looked back toward Nancy's house and spotted her staring at them. Nancy closed her curtain when she saw Anita staring back at her.

"Come on, let's get in the house," Anita said. She wrapped her arm around Aniya and walked home.

***

Nancy was sleeping when she woke up to the sound of a baby crying.

"Zhori!" she cried out as she sat up in her bed.

The crying continued. Nancy quickly removed her covers and jumped out of bed.

"Zhori!" Nancy yelled as she ran out of her room. "God, my baby!"

Nancy pushed her daughter's bedroom door open and said, "Zhori, mommy's here baby. Don't cry."

Nancy pulled the blankets off of the stuffed animals and the crying got louder. "Zhori, where are you?" she cried.

Nancy paused for a second and stared at the closet. She heard the crying again and opened the closet door.

"Oh no, my baby!" Nancy threw everything out of the closet, searching for the source of the sound.

There was no baby there. Nancy crawled out from the closet and cried heavily.

"I want my baby!" Nancy cried to herself as she slid down against the wall, falling to the floor.

There was a knock on Nancy's front door.

Nancy stopped crying and wiped the tears from her eyes. The knocking continued. Nancy got off of the floor and walked to the door.

When she opened the door, Aniya was standing there.

"Hi," Aniya said.

"Hi," Nancy replied hoarsely.

"Wow, are you okay? You kind of look ratchet."

"Ratchet?" Nancy asked with a confused look on her face.

"Yeah. Ratchet is the hood term for looking terrible," Aniya said before laughing.

Nancy laughed as well. "Ratchet, huh? Come on in here."

"I hope I'm not a bother coming over here like this."

"Oh, of course not. Come on, let me fix you something to eat."

Nancy and Aniya were in the kitchen. Aniya was eating her sandwich when she looked up and noticed Nancy was not touching her food. She was watching her eat instead.

"Is something wrong?" Aniya asked before she took a sip of her soda.

"I just had a meltdown," Nancy said, taking a deep breath.

"What's wrong?"

"I have so much frustration and anger. I'm still holding on to my child even though she is gone."

"That's understandable," Aniya responded.

"I don't know if it's because of guilt that I been holding on to. Knowing that it was I that caused the death of my child."

"I kind of took my frustration out on her room," Nancy said as she ran her hand through her hair.

Aniya put down her sandwich and said, "Come on, let's go."

"Go where?"

"Go clean your daughter's room."

"Oh no, of course not. I did it, I'll take care of it."

"Come on, I insist," Aniya said as she rose from the table.

"Okay, boss," Nancy laughed.

They walked down the hall and Nancy opened the door to her daughter's room.

"And you said you kind of took it out on your daughter's room," Aniya said as she looked at the wreckage.

Nancy just shrugged her shoulders.

As Aniya and Nancy sat on the floor picking up items, Nancy noticed Aniya staring at a baby blanket that was specially made. It was a pink and white blanket with the name Zhori stitched across the middle.

"It's a beautiful blanket, isn't it?" Nancy said as she admired it.

"It is," Aniya responded. She got quiet, lowering her head.

"Aniya, is there something wrong?"

"Yeah."

"What is it? You can tell me anything," Nancy said as she rubbed Aniya's hand.

"Well, I'm pregnant. And I'm scared," she said softly as she looked up hesitantly at Nancy.

Nancy acted as if she didn't already know the news.

"Honey, you're going to be just fine!" Nancy put her arm around her reassuringly.

"You're just saying that to make me feel better. You know I'm too young. My momma is, well, you know. I didn't finish school yet, I live in the ghetto, and the daddy of this child is moving away."

Nancy took a deep breath before starting, "Well Aniya, the damage is already done. Now it's time to focus and change your path. Yes, you should have waited, but your life doesn't end here."

Just then, Aniya's cell phone rang. She saw Malik's name on the screen and accepted the call. "Hi Malik," she said with joy in her voice. "Of course, I'll be right there." She hung up.

"I guess you are going see a special someone!" Nancy teased.

"Let me finish helping you first!"

"Oh, don't be silly. I've got this, you go on and have fun."

Aniya smiled as she and Nancy got up off of the floor.

"Thanks for listening," Aniya said before she began to walk off.

"Hey," Nancy started. "Just know that anytime you need me, I'm here for you. No matter what it is."

Aniya smiled and then walked off. She made it outside and saw Malik coming toward her from across the street.

"Malik!" she called as she ran in his direction. They hugged each other tightly.

"Hey, are you ready to take a ride?" he asked.

"Take a ride in what?"

Malik pointed across the street. A new car sat on the side of the road in front of her house.

"Oh, Malik! Is that yours?"

"It sure is, come on!" he said, taking her hand.

***

"Wow Malik, that was a nice ride," Aniya said after Malik pulled the car to a stop in front of his house.

"It's always a nice ride when I'm with you," he replied as he turned the car off.

"Did you forget something at home?"

"Why would I have forgotten something?" Malik asked as he winked at Aniya.

"Well, we're here in front your house."

"We're having lunch with my mom, grandma, and sister. I mean, if that's okay with you," he said before he kissed Aniya on the hand.

"What? Is this some kind of sick joke?"

"Of course not, Aniya. Why would I want to do something like that to you?"

"You know good and well your momma doesn't like me. Why would she want me to sit at her table?"

"Would you lighten up? I'm trying to spend as much time with you as I can and you're still complaining. You know what, if you want to go home, you can go," he said as he started the car up again.

"No, of course not. I want to stay," Aniya said softly.

Malik shut off his engine again. They both got out of the car and walked into his house.

"Well, well, look who's here! My handsome grandson and his pretty little girlfriend! Come here and give me a hug!" Silva said. She hugged Malik tightly before hugging Aniya.

"Thank you, you're so kind," Aniya said with a big smile on her face.

Malik's mother entered the living room. "Hi, honey. Glad you made it back," she said.

"Hey," Malik said before he kissed his mother on the head.

"Aniya," Malik's mother said, taking notice of her.

"Hello," Aniya replied cautiously.

"Well, lunch will be ready in just a minute. Hopefully your sister will be on time," his mother stated.

"Thanks, ma. Come on, Aniya," Malik said as he moved down the hall.

Aniya and Malik went to his room.

Coretta and Shania walked into the house, their arms filled with bags.

"If you buy anymore clothes, you won't be able to fit into your own room," Sandra said while laughing.

"Come on, Shania, let's go put this stuff away," Coretta said.

Shania and Coretta walked up to her room when Shania heard voices coming from Malik's room. His door was open just a crack. Shania and Coretta placed all the bags on her bed.

"I'm going to go to the restroom," Shania lied.

"Yeah girl, go right on ahead."

***

"So, when are you planning to tell your mom?" Aniya asked Malik.

"Tell my mom that we are expecting a child?" Malik responded.

"Well, yes."

Shania crept up to listen by the door.

"Why do you want to tell her so bad?" Malik asked in frustration.

"I just want her to—" Aniya took a deep breath and stopped herself from saying anymore.

"You just want her to like you because you're pregnant. That just won't work," he said.

Shania put her hand over her mouth to cover her gasp. At that moment, Coretta stepped out of her room and saw her friend eavesdropping. Coretta stood there quietly with her arms folded, watching Shania.

"I told you, in due time I will tell her. But right now let's just keep everything good. She's willing to have lunch with you. I mean, that's a start," Malik said. "Now give me a hug."

"Everything will work out eventually," he said as he held her tightly.

Coretta went back into her room before Shania could see her.

Shania walked quietly back to Coretta's room.

"You back from the restroom?" Coretta said to Shania as she reentered the room.

"Yes, of course," Shania replied nervously. She began messing with the bags on the bed as Coretta just watched her. Coretta knew something was up with Shania, but she couldn't put her finger on it. Why was Shania spying on Malik?

***

Everyone was sitting around in the backyard. The table was covered with hotdogs, burgers, punch, cakes, and veggies. Malik, Aniya, Silva, and Malik's mother were taking a seat around the picnic table.

"Oh, honey, you did such a wonderful job. This food looks delicious," Silva said as she poured punch into her glass.

"Thanks ma, I really tried," Malik's mother said.

Coretta and Shania walked outside to join the rest of the party.

"Well, look who's joining us!" Silva said loudly.

Everyone looked up at Coretta and Shania as they walked toward them. Aniya stared at Shania as she ate her burgers and fries.

"Hi, Grandma," Coretta said before she kissed Silva on the cheek.

"It seems like you forgot to mention Shania was coming," Aniya muttered to Malik under her breath.

Malik continued to smile and ignored Aniya's comment.

"Hi, Mrs. Silva," Shania said. She kissed Silva on the forehead.

"I didn't know she was going to be here," Malik mumbled back.

"Nice to see you, baby," Silva responded.

"Malik," Shania began as she gave him a flirtatious look.

"Shania," Malik said, clearing his throat. "It's nice to see you."

"Aniya," Shania muttered as she took a seat at the table, not even looking in Aniya's direction.

"Hi," Aniya said plainly.

"Let's say grace, shall we?" Malik's mother said. Everyone bowed their heads.

"Aniya, would you say grace, please?" Silva asked.

"Okay, I guess," Aniya said uneasily.

"Go on," Silva encouraged. Aniya bowed her head and closed her eyes tightly.

"Dear God, thank you for this food you have placed before us," Aniya prayed.

As Aniya continued to say grace, Shania rubbed her leg against Malik's under the table. Malik looked up and saw Shania blowing him a kiss. Malik winked at her.

"Amen," Aniya finished.

"Amen," everyone repeated, opening their eyes. Everyone began passing the dishes around, piling their plates high with food.

"You know, it's funny how we couldn't pull you two away from each other as kids with all that puppy love. Yet you still managed to be friends after all this time," Silva said.

Malik choked on his punch.

"Oh, I didn't know Malik when we were younger, Mrs. Silva," Aniya explained.

"I wasn't talking about you, honey. I'm talking about Shania over here."

Aniya slowly put down her hotdog. She felt nothing but shame and anger.

"It feels like it was just yesterday," Shania said.

Aniya stared at Malik in silence.

"I thought you two just met," Aniya said to him. "I thought you said she was a new girl just coming to town."

"Oh, was that what he told you?" Coretta said.

"Aniya, you're making this seem bigger than what it actually is," Malik stated.

"Oh child, please. That was kiddy love, they were just kids. It's nothing to get your brains all worked up over. I'm sorry I brought it up," Silva said with a frown.

"No momma, you're fine. Come on, I didn't make all this food for nothing. Everybody eat up!" Malik's mother tried to change the conversation.

"Excuse me, I'm not feeling so well. May I use the restroom?" Aniya asked, yearning to get away.

It was silent.

"Of course," Malik said, breaking the silence. He lowered his head and took a deep breath.

"I don't know what's she's going to do when you leave for college in the fall." Malik's mother said before she took a bite of her burger.

"What you mean by that, mom?" Malik asked as he pushed his plate away, folding his arms on the table.

"Malik, you're going to be surrounded by girls who are far more mature than that one. I mean, eventually you will—"

"I will what? Make your wish come true and leave Aniya?"

"Well, she is right, Malik. I mean look at her, acting like a child," Coretta said.

"All right! All right! We are a family. There's no need for this. Aniya is Malik's girlfriend. That's who he loves. It really doesn't matter what anyone else thinks," Silva said.

"I hope I'm not causing any trouble," Shania said with fake innocence.

"Of course you're not. Everybody is making this bigger than what it really is," Malik said reassuringly.

"Or maybe someone is not seeing it for what it really is," Sandra said as she took a sip of punch.

"Maybe I should go talk with her," Shania said as she rose up from her chair.

Aniya was in the restroom vomiting. Shania walked up to the bathroom door and knocked.

"Aniya, are you okay in there?" Shania asked quietly.

"I'm fine," Aniya said before vomiting again.

"It doesn't sound like it."

Aniya didn't say a word.

"Well, listen. I have to talk to you about something, so I'll be out here waiting for you."

Aniya finally got off of the floor and got a towel to clean herself up. She went to the sink and turned on the cold water. She looked up in the mirror at herself.

"What have you done to yourself, Aniya," she thought to herself.

She put the towel under the running water. She wiped her face slowly as tears ran down her face. She finally came out the restroom and entered the kitchen with her head down, bumping into Shania. Aniya immediately looked up.

"Oh Shania, I'm sorry," Aniya said nervously.

Shania folded her arms.

"Finished puking out your guts?" Shania said with a smirk.

"Look, I don't have time for this," Aniya said as she tried to pass Shania, but Shania stood in her way.

"You know, I've been thinking. Since we haven't been properly introduced, I thought I should let you know I'm not just the new girl. I dated Malik before you did. Sorry you've been lied to," Shania said, not sorry in the slightest.

"Well, it doesn't mean anything now. Would you please move?"

"I know your little secret," Shania said, moving closer to Aniya. "And let me tell you something, you're in for a rude awakening. Malik is about to leave and he will not be thinking about you. You know Malik's mother dislikes you. Just imagine when she finds out! She will hate your guts from trying to trap her son!"

"I'm not trying to trap anybody, so stop bumping your gums about what you don't understand! Now, move!" Aniya shouted as she pushed Shania out of the way.

"Don't you ever bump me again!" Shania yelled.

Coretta entered the kitchen, but neither Shania nor Aniya noticed her.

Shania pushed Aniya with all of her force, knocking her into the table. Aniya screamed as she lost her balance, falling to the floor. Coretta's mouth opened in a gasp. Malik ran into the kitchen with his mother and grandmother.

"What is going on here?" he yelled.

Coretta quickly turned around to look at her brother.

Shania turned around with a smile on her face and said, "Oh, clumsy Aniya here just had a fall."

Malik ran over to Aniya.

"Oh my God! Are you okay, Aniya?" Malik's grandmother asked.

"She pushed me, Malik!" Aniya said as tears rolled down her face.

"What, are you serious?" Malik said angrily. Malik got up and grabbed Shania by the neck.

Sandra screamed, "Malik, let her go!"

"Are you crazy? You could've hurt her!" Malik yelled.

Shania glared into Malik's eyes.

"Malik, let her go!" Sandra shouted.

"Listen to your mother!" Silva said.

"Malik, please!" Aniya cried as she sat on the floor.

Malik slowly let Shania go and Coretta ran off crying.

"You see what you did? You scared your sister!" Sandra said.

Shania was holding her neck, gasping for breath.

"Baby, are you all right?" Malik asked as he helped Aniya off the floor.

"I'll go check on Coretta," Malik's mom said as she walked out of the room.

"Oh God, what is going on here? The devil has got a hold on this house and I rebuke him in the name of Jesus right this instant!" Silva shouted.

"I think I better leave. I can't stay here another second," said Shania as she stopped and turned toward Malik. "You will regret ever putting your hands on me."

Chapter Eight

The next day at work, Malik's mother dressed in a tight black skirt that stopped at the knees, and a dressy purple top. Malik's mother entered the big open office smiling while humming a tune. Everyone in the office looked at Malik's mother. It was so silent, a cotton ball could hit the floor and it would make a noise. Some receptionists were sitting, while others were getting a cup of coffee.

"Well, don't just sit there like bumps on a log! Let's put some smiles on our faces! The sun is out, my son is about to leave for college, and I'm one proud momma!" Malik's mother shouted as she did a little dance. "It's a new day. Let's be glad and rejoice in it!"

No one smiled or said a word.

"What's wrong with y'all? Y'all look like somebody just died."

No one said a word and some lowered their heads.

"Oh, Hell with you people!" Sandra said as she headed over to her work booth.

"What is this?" Sandra said. "Who did this?"

Sandra started pulling down papers that were taped all over her booth. Everyone watched Malik's mother in silence.

"Oh God, this can't be true!" Malik's mother cried out loud.

***

Aniya was sitting at Nancy's house on the couch eating chocolate cake when Nancy entered the living room.

"Enjoying it?" asked Nancy, she smiled and rocked back and forth in excitement, holding her hands behind her back.

"Oh, thank you so much, Mrs. Nancy. This was exactly what I needed!" Aniya said.

"Look what I bought the other day!" Nancy said as she removed her hands from her back, holding a pink and brown baby outfit.

"Wow, it's adorable! I love it. Who's it for?" asked Aniya.

"Zhori of course, who else?" Nancy said matter-of-factly. She smiled and admired the outfit in her hands.

"You mean your daughter that died?" Aniya asked as she stared at Nancy.

Nancy stared back at Aniya as the happiness left her face. It turned into anger.

"Nancy, are you okay? Did I say something wrong?" Aniya asked as she rose off of the sofa.

"Don't you ever speak that way in my home!" Nancy yelled.

"I'm sorry, Nancy! What did I say to offend you?"

"My daughter is alive!"

"No, she's not. You said she died."

Nancy began to get red in the face as she stared at Aniya.

"Look Nancy, you're really starting to freak me out," Aniya said as she started to back away slowly.

A loud knock came from the front door. Nancy and Aniya continued to stare at one another. Another loud knock sounded and someone shouted Aniya's name.

"I think that's my mom calling. I have to go. I hope you can get through these hard times, Nancy," Aniya said. She passed in front Nancy and headed toward the door.

Nancy just stared without saying a word as Aniya opened her front door.

"Baby, come here. We have to go!" Anita said urgently. She grabbed Aniya by the hand and pulled her out of Nancy's house.

"What do you mean, momma?" Aniya asked nervously.

Anita continued to walk while she pulled on Aniya's hand. Aniya yanked her hand free and Anita stopped walking. She turned around quickly to face Aniya.

"Why must you be so difficult, child?" Anita shouted.

Nancy appeared in her doorway, watching Anita and Aniya.

"I'm not taking another step until you tell me what's going on!" Aniya demanded.

Anita started to cry.

"Momma, what's wrong? You're scaring me. Why are you crying?" Aniya asked as she wrapped her arms around her mother tightly.

Aniya then heard footsteps coming up behind them.

"Yea, that's right, cry your eyes out. You should be ashamed of yourself!" a woman's voice said. It was Aniya's grandmother, Martha.

"Grandma?" Aniya said, stunned to see her.

"Oh, my baby! Look how much you've grown! I missed you so much!" said Martha.

"Oh, Grandma, I miss you!" Aniya said as she and her grandma hugged tightly.

"God, I miss you," Martha whispered into Aniya's hair.

Anita continued to cry beside them.

Martha and Aniya let go of each other and Martha turned to stare at Anita.

"And you. I couldn't be more disappointed of you than I am right now, Nita," Martha said as she pointed her finger at Anita.

"What did momma do?" Aniya said sadly.

"I'll tell you!" said Martha sternly, one hand on her hip and the other pointed at Anita.

Anita lowered her head.

"Her addiction to drugs doesn't only affect her, but her loved ones as well. She can't keep food in her house, she messes with worthless men, and she can't keep a job to save her life!" shouted Martha. She walked up to Anita and glared at her.

"And the reason I'm so mad is because it took all I had to raise you, Nita. You could be so much better," said Martha. "Nita, you want to tell her the reason I'm down here?"

"No, ma'am," Anita said quietly.

Martha turned to face Aniya.

"Because you have just become homeless, that's why. And I refuse to let a grandchild of mine live on the streets," Martha said with anger and sadness in her voice.

"Grandma, what are you talking about? We live right there across the street," Aniya said.

"Honey, there's something I have to tell you," Anita said as she reached out to hold Aniya's hands. "I lost our apartment, Niya."

"You what?" Aniya cried as she pulled her hands away from Anita. "Momma!"

Nancy placed one hand over her heart and one over her mouth as she continued listening from afar.

"Come on and pack your things, we're leaving this town," said Martha.

"Momma, you coming?" asked Aniya.

Anita began to fidget with her hands and said, "No baby, I'm afraid momma can't go on this trip."

"Momma, I'm not leaving you!" Aniya said as she ran to hug Anita.

"I'm afraid you have no choice," said Martha.

Aniya unwrapped her arms from around her mother and looked at her mom as tears steadily flowed down her face.

It's got quiet before Nancy walked across the street to Aniya and her family.

"Please, let me take her," Nancy offered.

Aniya, Anita, and Martha all looked at her.

"Really? You would let me stay with you?" Aniya asked.

Nancy grabbed both of Aniya's hands and smiled at her.

"It would be my pleasure," Nancy said.

"Mom, is it okay if I stay with Mrs. Nancy?" Aniya asked as she turned to look at her mother.

"I don't think that's a good idea. You need to be with family and we don't know a thing about this stranger," Anita said angrily.

"You know, baby, this is the first time I agree with your mother. You need to be with family where you can receive the love and care you need," said Martha.

"But granny, mommy, I really like Nancy," Aniya said with a pout.

"Aniya, you're going with grandma and that's final!" Anita said bluntly.

"Please, hear me out," Nancy said as she let go of Aniya's hands to stand in front of Anita.

"Think about it. Aniya has already been through enough already, it will be good for her to stay around her friends. We can do things together, like attend church functions. You know, I'm a counselor as well," Nancy said as she turned to Martha. "Maybe I can help her."

Martha didn't say a word as she took a look at Aniya. She then looked back at Nancy.

"Listen," Nancy continued. "If this does not work out, you can take her back without me saying a word. Please, I want to help."

"Please," added Aniya.

Anita and Martha looked at each other. They spoke with their eyes.

"Well, I guess it wouldn't hurt to try it for a while," said Martha.

"Yes!" Aniya cried as she went to hug her grandma.

***

Malik's mom rushed into Silva's arms crying, "Malik! Malik!"

"Child, what's wrong with you?" Silva asked her daughter. Silva let go of her daughter and walked with her into the living room, wiping her hands off with a kitchen towel.

"I'm going to kill him!" Malik's mom shouted as she took off running up the stairs. Silva ran up the stairs after Malik's mom.

"Malik! Malik!" Malik's mom cried as she burst through his door.

No one was there.

Malik's mom started to knock pictures and awards off of Malik's dresser as she screamed. Silva stepped into the room and immediately put her hand over her heart. She gasped as she watched her daughter destroy Malik's room.

"Child, what is going on with you?" Silva shouted.

Malik's mother continued throwing things as she screamed, "How could you do this to me? How could you Malik?"

She fell to the floor as Silva leaned down to gently wrap her arms around her.

"Baby, what has troubled you?" Silva asked softly.

Malik's mother dug into her pocket, pulled out a piece of paper, and handed it to her mother. Silva opened the letter slowly and read it in silence.

Malik entered the room.

"What's going on here?" Malik said, upset and confused.

Silva and Malik's mom immediately turned in Malik's direction. Malik's mom's eyes were as red as fire.

"You!" Malik's mom shouted as she struggled to get off the floor.

Silva got up as well. Malik's mom rushed over to him and began hitting him and screaming incoherently at the same time.

"Momma, what's your problem?" Malik yelled as he grabbed her wrists to keep her hands from reaching him.

"Let me go!" she shouted as she tried to tug her hands away from him.

Silva tried to hold her back and said, "Okay, just calm down, baby. Take a deep breath."

"Momma, what's going on?" Malik shouted as he continued to hold onto her.

"Let go of me, Malik, before I kill you!" she shouted back.

"Woman, what has gotten into you?" Malik shouted as he stared into his mother's eyes.

Malik's mother snatched the paper from Silva's hands and threw it at Malik before she walked out of the room, leaving him to read it for himself.

***

Aniya and Jeff were sitting at the kitchen table eating.

"So, how do you think you're going to like living with Nancy and I?" Jeff asked as he took a bite of his broccoli.

"I think I will love it here," Aniya said as she took a sip of her juice.

"Great, cause we love to have you here," Jeff said as he gave Aniya a smile.

Nancy was in the guest bedroom searching through Aniya's belongings. Aniya's phone rang and Nancy grabbed it to look at the caller ID. She noticed it was Malik calling.

"Soon you will be out the picture," Nancy said to herself menacingly before rejecting the call.

Nancy threw Aniya's cellphone on the bed. She then continued digging through Aniya's things when the phone beeped from it's place on the bed.

"I'll be damned Malik! Would you give it a rest? She's in my care now," Nancy muttered to herself as she grabbed the phone again.

Nancy opened the message. It said: "Aniya this is not fucking funny, it's important. Now answer the damn phone!"

Nancy deleted the message and threw the phone on the floor, causing the battery to pop out of it.

Nancy continued going through Aniya's things when she saw a letter fall onto the floor. She reached down to open it up but froze when she heard footsteps come up behind her.

"What are you doing?" Aniya said as she folded her arms. She was standing in the doorway of the room.

Nancy slowly turned around with a smile.

"Okay, you caught me," Nancy said as she put the letter behind her back. "I was going to give them to you later, but no time is better than the present." Nancy reached into her pocket and pulled out a small box. She held out her hand to Aniya.

"What is it?" Aniya said as she took the box from Nancy's hand.

"Well, why don't you see for yourself?"

Aniya opened up the gift box.

"Well, what do you think?" Nancy asked.

"Oh my God, they're beautiful," Aniya said as a smile appeared on her face.

"I thought you would like them," Nancy said with a smile.

"I have never received a beautiful gift like this before," Aniya said as she took the diamond earrings out of the box.

"They're just a token to show you how much we appreciate you staying with us," Nancy said.

"Thank you," Aniya said as she and Nancy hugged tightly.

"Well, I'll let you get comfortable," Nancy said as she began walking out of the room. Nancy was closing the door when Aniya began to speak.

"Nancy," Aniya said. "I'm sorry for all the attitude. I guess I'm going through—"

"It's all right," Nancy said, cutting her off as she smiled.

***

Aniya stepped out of the shower and put on her bathrobe. She blotted her hair dry while looking at herself in the mirror. She put down the towel and picked up the gift box from the dresser.

Nancy quietly opened the door to Aniya's room and stared. Aniya opened the box and took the earrings out, placing them in her ears one by one. She admired herself in the mirror.

"They're gorgeous on you," Nancy said from the doorway.

Aniya jumped as she quickly turned in Nancy's direction.

"Oh God, you scared me. I didn't hear you come in," Aniya said.

"I just wanted to tell you there's a church event going on tomorrow evening. Would like to join me?" Nancy asked.

Aniya smiled and replied, "Sure, I would love that."

"Great! Well, goodnight," Nancy said.

"Goodnight," Aniya replied.

***

Nancy went in the kitchen to drink coffee with one of her friends that had come over to visit.

"I'm so glad you came so we could catch up. I really miss you," Nancy said as she placed her hand on top of Marcy's.

"Me too. Let's make a promise to take time out of our busy schedules to have girl time!" Marcy said with a big smile on her face.

Nancy and Marcy both laughed.

***

Aniya was getting ready in her room when she noticed her cellphone on the floor without the battery in it.

"Oh hell no," Aniya said angrily.

***

"So, I know it's been a year, but are you doing okay?" Marcy asked gently as she lowered her head.

"You mean the loss of my child?" asked Nancy as she cleared her throat.

"Yeah," Marcy said in a soft tone.

"You know, I'm taking it one day at a time," Nancy said. "Besides, God is going to bless me with a baby real soon."

Marcy looked up at Nancy with a confused face and asked, "Are you pregnant?"

At that moment, Aniya came rushing into the kitchen.

"What did you do to my phone?" Aniya cried out angrily.

Nancy and Marcy turned quickly to look at Aniya.

"Excuse me?" Nancy said.

"Where did you hide the battery for my cellphone?" Aniya shouted.

"Now, just calm down and tell me what you're talking about," Nancy said as she slowly rose from her chair.

"Don't play coy with me, you took the battery from my phone!"

Marcy put down her coffee as she watched Aniya and Nancy argue.

"Why would you say a thing like that Aniya? I mean, why would I take your battery?"

"Yeah, why would you?" Aniya asked.

"Listen, I'll buy you another one. It's no big deal," Nancy said.

Aniya took off walking toward the kitchen door.

"Where are you going, Aniya?"

"I'm out of here," Aniya said as she walked through the door.

"Well, I think that's my cue. I better get going," Marcy said as she rose from her chair.

"I'm so sorry, Marcy. I didn't mean for—" Nancy said before Marcy waved a hand to stop her.

"It's quite all right. Typical teenagers," Marcy said with a small smile.

Nancy smiled back and waved at Marcy as she left. Nancy then took a deep breath as her smile dropped.

"I am not about to put up with this nonsense. Not today," Nancy mumbled to herself.

***

"Remember, if we repent sincerely from our hearts, God will forgive. He is a loving and forgiving God. And with that love, my brothers and sisters, stay blessed," said the Preacher as his sermon ended.

Everyone stood to leave and Nancy and Aniya walked out of the church together.

They stopped in front the church's doorway to say goodbye to Nancy's friends. Aniya stood there with a sour attitude and folded arms.

"Hey!" Malik shouted as pushed through the crowd. "Aniya!" Malik shouted once again as he continued to fight his way through the crowd.

Aniya quickly turned at the sound of his voice.

"Malik!" she called as she started running in his direction.

"Come here, now!" Malik shouted as he grabbed Aniya by the arm and pulled her through the crowd.

"Hey, watch it Malik! You're hurting me!"

"Why did you tell my mom about the baby? Didn't we have an agreement that we were going to tell her when the time was right?" Malik shouted as his face became red.

Nancy noticed the commotion between Malik and Aniya and began to walk in their direction.

"What are you talking about, Malik? I never said anything to your mom!" Aniya said as she shook her head in confusion.

"No, that's right, you didn't 'tell' her. You showed her in a letter and embarrassed her in front of everyone at her job!" Malik said in a rage as his hands continued to fly in the air.

"Malik, I don't have a clue about what you're talking about. I don't even know where your mom works!" Aniya shouted back. "And why was she embarrassed? She's going to be a grandma whether she likes it or not!" She began to walk off when Malik pulled her arm back.

"You listen here!" Malik said as he ground his teeth together.

"Let go of her!" Nancy said as she walked up and tugged on Malik's shirt. "I will not let you talk to her that way. And let me tell you something, it took two to make this baby. Whether you or your mom are okay or not okay with it, this baby will be born. And guess what?

I will make sure you never lay eyes on it!" Nancy said as she got right in Malik's face, glaring into his eyes.

"It ain't mine anyway!" Malik yelled as he glared at Aniya before walking off.

Aniya started crying.

***

"Okay Aniya, we have to move faster than that or we will be late for school," Nancy said as she stood in Aniya's doorway.

Aniya rubbed her stomach, not wanting to move.

"Aniya, you're going to feel like this. You're halfway through your pregnancy now. Come on and eat breakfast before we're late."

"Don't you understand? I don't want to do anything! I have a mom who doesn't even call me, my baby's daddy hasn't talked to me in months, and he never even let me know when he left for college! I'm big, pregnant, and don't want to live anymore!" Aniya said as she began to cry.

"Aniya, you stop this nonsense right now, and I mean right now! You don't need anyone else. I'm here for you," Nancy said as she entered the room. Nancy knelt down by the bed where Aniya was sitting. "I'm going to take care of you and this baby."

Aniya took a deep breath as she stared Nancy in the face and said, "You're not my mother."

Nancy slapped Aniya across the face.

Aniya quickly held the side of her face and gaped at Nancy.

"Listen, you ungrateful, smart-mouthed brat. Your mother can't stay off the crack, let alone take care herself. If she would do what she was supposed to as a mother, you wouldn't be here."

Aniya continued to cry.

"Now dry the tears and come eat this breakfast!" Nancy demanded as she quickly stood to her feet.

"Is everything all right?" Jeff asked as he slowly pushed Aniya's door open.

Nancy quickly fixed her dress and said, "Sure, honey. Everything is just peachy."

Aniya lowered her head and turned away from Jeff.

"Okay. Well, I'm headed off to work," Jeff said while looking at Aniya. "Aniya are you okay?"

"Of course, just a little pregnancy hormones taking place," Nancy said nervously with a fake smile. "Right, Aniya?"

"Yes," Aniya said softly as she kept her head down.

"You're going to be just fine, Aniya," Jeff said.

Aniya didn't respond and Jeff walked away from the door.

"Honey, will you be back for dinner?" Nancy called after him.

"I will have to work late, don't wait up for me!" Jeff called back loudly.

***

Aniya was in the kitchen sitting at the table taking a bite of her buttered toast while Nancy chopped up a pineapple. The mailman passed the kitchen window before he stopped in front of Nancy's home. Nancy watched the mailman for a moment before she put her knife down.

"I'll be back," Nancy said quietly. She then swiftly walked out the door to the mailman.

"Hi," said the mailman with a smile.

"Hi," Nancy said as she smiled back. "What do you have for me today?"

Aniya walked over to the window as she watched Nancy and the mailman.

"Just this right here," said the mailman, handing a few letters to Nancy. She flipped through the mail as he turned to walk away.

"Wait! Hold on one minute!" Nancy called after the mailman as her smile quickly disappeared. She began tugging on the mailman's shirt for him to turn around.

Aniya continued to watch suspiciously from the window.

"What did I tell you about delivering these letters to my house?" Nancy said as she waved the letter in the mailman's face.

"I don't know how it got mixed up in there. I'm sorry for the mishap," he replied cautiously.

"You see, that's what's wrong with you young people. You don't know how to follow simple instructions. Keep that crap out of your ears and a mishap would not take place!" Nancy shouted as she pulled his ear buds off his shoulders.

The mailman put his ear buds in his pocket and looked up at the house. He noticed Aniya staring at him from the kitchen window.

"Now, you take this back!" Nancy said as she pushed the letter against his chest.

The mailman continued to watch Aniya and Aniya gently rubbed her pregnant belly.

"No, better than that! I'll take it. I can't trust you," Nancy said as she glared at the mailman's face. She noticed he was watching her house.

Nancy looked at her house, but Aniya had left the window. Nancy walked off from the mailman. She entered the kitchen and spotted no one.

"Aniya!" she called out.

When Nancy turned around, Aniya passed by her heading for the door. Nancy jumped.

"Oh gosh, you scared me!" Nancy said as she placed her hand over her heart.

Aniya did not say a word as she continued to walk with one backpack strap on her shoulder.

"Are you ready, sweetie?" Nancy asked.

"I'm walking to school," Aniya said as she exited the kitchen. She then immediately took off running out of the house. She stopped running when she reached the end of the driveway. She looked both ways as Nancy watched her from the window.

Aniya took off in the direction of the mailman, screaming to him as she tried to run while holding her belly. The mailman looked in his rearview mirror and noticed Aniya bent over, holding her stomach. He immediately stopped and jumped out the truck, running over to her.

"Hey! Are you okay?" he asked her.

Aniya was taking deep breaths as she slowly raised her eyes to look at him.

"Yes, I'm fine thank you. Listen, have you been receiving mail from my mother, Anita?"

The mailman just stood there in silence as he started fidgeting with his hands. "Huh? Excuse me, I receive mail all the time. It's hard to recall all the mail I receive.

The mailman slowly turned around without saying a word and began walking toward his truck. Aniya walked after him.

"Where are they?" she asked. "'Cause I never received one. It just doesn't seem like my mother would just forget about me. Her name Is Anita Cooper. And it should be addressed to me, Aniya Cooper."

Aniya and the mailman made it to his truck.

"Listen," he started. "She must be hiding them in the house—that's all I can tell you."

"How do you know that for a fact?"

He took a deep breath as he got back in his truck. Aniya stared at the mailman and he stared back, hesitant.

"Nancy would always say she's tired of me bringing junk mail," he said. "She would throw mail in the trash with me standing right there. I didn't think anything of it because she always had a bunch of mail, there was bound to be junk. But on another occasion, the only piece of mail I had to deliver to her was a letter from Anita Cooper. Nancy threw it in the trash."

"I think I just might have something for you," said the mailman as he reached over and took the top off of a box. He held the letter out to her. "This was the letter from your mom." I don't know how this one slipped past me.

"Oh, thank you so much! I truly, truly appreciate it!" Aniya said happily as she grabbed the letter.

"Glad I can be a help," he said before starting the car and driving off. Aniya stuck the letter in her backpack and zipped it up. However, part of the letter was sticking out of her bag.

"You can't just leave like that," Nancy said, coming up behind Aniya.

Aniya jumped and turned quickly to face Nancy. She stood in silence.

"Turn around," Nancy demanded. Aniya hesitated and realized her mother's letter was sticking out of her bag.

"Aniya, would you turn around?" Nancy said again. Aniya slowly turned around and Nancy grabbed Aniya's hair and put it in a ponytail.

"There, you look perfect with this new hair accessory I bought you," Nancy said happily as she placed the hair accessory in Aniya's Hair.

Nancy then noticed the letter sticking out of Aniya's book bag. Aniya nervously played with her fingers as Nancy reached for the letter. Right before she could grab it, a car honked the horn at her.

"Nancy!" a lady shouted as she waved at her, turning in her driveway. Nancy waved back, forgetting about the letter.

"Well, you get going to school before you're late," Nancy said before heading over to meet her friend.

Aniya took a deep breath and began walking to school. She took the letter out of her bag and read it, hearing her mother's voice in her mind.

Dear Aniya,

I've written you before, but it's clear to me now that you don't want me involved in your life. I'm sorry, but you should understand that a mother never gives up on her child.

You are pregnant with my grandchild, and I think of you and the baby constantly. Sometimes that's all that makes me want to get better. But then I remember how much you resent me as a mother and I just want to give up. If I don't have you, then there's no need to go on.

I hope one day you can forgive me. I'm on the path to knowing who God really is and what power He has. I hope to see you as soon as I get better.

Kiss your hand and touch your stomach. Tell my grandbaby it's from grandma. Well, time is short. I love you, and stay strong.

Love always,

Momma

Tears began to roll down Aniya's face.

Aniya hid behind some bushes when she noticed Nancy was driving in her direction, heading to work. Once she passed, Aniya quickly walked back to the house. She grabbed the hidden key out of the mailbox and went inside to Nancy's room. She began searching through her drawers. After finding nothing there, she went into the closet.

***

"Oh no, I forgot my files!" Nancy said to herself. She began turning her car around to return home.

***

Aniya accidentally knocked into a box that fell to the floor. A bundle of letters fell out. She stared for a second before she bent down slowly. These were all of the letters from her mother that she never received.

***

Nancy entered the house and muttered, "Where did I leave my briefcase?"

Aniya heard Nancy enter the house and shoved the letters in her backpack. Nancy opened the bedroom door and Aniya stood quietly in the closet, looking at Nancy through the shutters.

Nancy noticed her drawers were open and began looking around to see if someone was in the house. She put her hand on the knob of the closet and Aniya slowly moved toward the back of the closet. Nancy turned the knob, but before she pulled open the door, the house phone rang. Nancy took her hand off of the closet door and left the room as Aniya took a deep breath.

"Hi, honey," Nancy said, smiling while she was on the phone.

Aniya crept out of the closet and noticed some money on top of Nancy's dresser. She grabbed it and snuck out the window. Aniya made it out before Nancy walked back into her room. However, Nancy noticed a breeze entering through the crack of her window. She walked to her window and looked out of it. Aniya was bent down on the ground under the window out of Nancy's view.

***

That night, Aniya tossed and turned in her sleep.

Nancy opened Aniya's door slowly and saw her lying on her back. Pleased that she was sleeping, Nancy left to go back to her room.

Aniya woke up and went to put the hidden key back into the mailbox. Once the key was back, Aniya crept back into her room.

Nancy heard noises coming from the front of the house, so she left her room and opened the front door. She checked the mailbox, making sure the hidden key was still in its place before putting it back in the mailbox and going back into the house.

***

Aniya got off the city bus, paying the driver before she stepped out.

She stared at the sign of the college dorm.

She began walking down the sidewalk, wobbling as she went. Aniya entered one of the college buildings with one hand on the strap of her book bag. She was walking down the hallways looking lost when a girl stopped her.

"Excuse me," said the girl as she touched Aniya's shoulder. Aniya turned around. "Do you need help finding something?"

"I'm looking for Malik Telman. He plays football, but you may not know him," Aniya answered.

"Of course I know him! he's on the football team," said the girl. "He's one of the best players!"

Aniya gave her a fake smile uninterested in the extra info.

"He's in a physics class right now, but he and the other football players usually get together and hang out in the student lounge afterward. I'm sure you can find him there."

"Thank you," Aniya said softly.

"Are you his sister?"

"A friend," Aniya responded.

"Yea, sure," she said sarcastically. "Well, I better get going before I'm late for my next class."

Mommy Help Me

After the girl left, Aniya walked around until she found the student lounge. A bunch of boys were making noise and laughing together. When Aniya turned the corner, she spotted Malik with a group of football players and cheerleaders. She stood at a distance and watched in silence.

"Malik, where are you taking me tonight?" asked a cheerleader as she walked up to Malik, rubbing his chest up and down.

The other boys on the football team hooted and whistled.

Aniya turned around and started walking away.

"Jasmine, you know the spot," Malik said before he kissed her on the lips. "Well boys, I have a physics class to get to." The cheerleaders giggled together and the football laughed.

Aniya bent over and leaned on the wall. She was holding her stomach in pain with her head lowered. Malik noticed her bent over and slowly approach her, not realizing who it was.

"Hey, are you okay?" Malik asked as he placed his hand on the girl's shoulder. When she looked up at Malik, he stared at her in shock.

"Aniya."

Aniya didn't say a word as she stared into Malik's eyes.

"Hey," he said roughly as he grabbed her by the arm. "What are you doing here?" He started moving down the hall while looking around, making sure no one spotted them.

"Let go of me!" Aniya said as she tried to yank her arm free.

They stopped at the end of the hall as it cleared up and Malik let go of her arm.

"What's wrong with you?" she asked angrily, rubbing her arm.

"What's wrong is you showing up out of thin air, big and pregnant, and you ask me what's wrong!" Malik said while grinding his teeth together.

"Listen, I need help Malik!" she pleaded.

"And you come all the way here when you need help?"

"Malik! Please, I need you right now!"

Malik stared at her for a second before taking a breath, rubbing his head with his hand.

"Are you hungry?" he finally asked.

***

Malik and Aniya were at a burger joint across from the campus. Aniya bit into her burger when she looked up and noticed Malik watching her. She quickly put down her burger wiped her face with a napkin.

"What's wrong? Are you not hungry? You haven't even touched your burger," Aniya said as she placed the napkin at the side of her plate.

"You never answered my calls, you changed your number, and you wrote me a letter telling me I'm not the father and that you don't want to have anything to do with me. And yet, here you are," Malik said sadly.

"What? I couldn't find my phone battery so Nancy bought me another phone. And I never wrote you any letter. I don't have a clue what you are talking about," Aniya said as her face turned red.

"Aniya, I was calling to apologize for what I had said to you. I tried to reconcile but I couldn't get in touch with you when I called. Plus, I went by Nancy's. She told me you and the baby will have nothing to do with me. She slammed the door in my face."

"Malik, I think Nancy has it out for me!" Aniya cried. "I think she only wants me for my child!"

"Your child?"

Aniya paused for a second before saying, "Our child, Malik."

"Aniya, are you sure this baby is mine?" he asked hesitantly.

"Malik, I swear this is your child," Aniya said as she put her hand on top of his. "I miss you."

"I miss you too, Aniya," Malik said. "Listen, you can stay in my dorm room so you can rest."

***

Aniya entered Malik's dorm.

"I have a roommate, so excuse his side. He believes this is a barnyard instead of a dorm room," Malik said as he and Aniya giggled.

Malik held Aniya's hands as they took a seat on his bed. "So, Nancy's giving you a hard time, huh?"

"Malik, if anything ever happens to me, promise me you'll take care of our daughter."

"Daughter," Malik said with a smile.

"I wish you could've been there when I found out," Aniya said.

"I'm sorry," Malik said as he wrapped his arms around Aniya.

There was a knock on the door.

"Malik," said a guy as he opened the door. "Whoa!" He quickly backed out of the room when he saw the two of them on the bed.

"Nah, it's all right," said Malik as he rose up from the bed.

"Can I holla at you for a minute?" asked the boy.

"Sure," Malik said. He then turned to Aniya and said, "I will be right back. You just stay put."

"Okay," she responded.

Malik left the room and Aniya got off the bed. She began looking around at all the pictures on the wall with Malik and his crew. Aniya then came to a picture of Malik and a cheerleader kissing. She looked closely and noticed it was the same girl Malik was kissing in the lounge. Aniya sadly lowered her head.

Just then, Malik's phone rang on the bed.

Aniya walked up to the bed and saw Shania's picture on the screen along with the name, Shania. Aniya slowly picked up the phone and hit the answer button. Aniya put the phone to her ear.

"Malik, baby, I forgot my underwear under the bed," said Shania as she let out a flirty giggle. "You know I don't want your roommate to see them. You know how he can be," Shania laughed so much as Aniya stayed silent. A tear fell down her face.

"Hello? Malik? Malik are you there?" asked Shania.

Aniya let the phone hit the floor.

"Malik, this is not funny. Say something!" said Shania. Aniya slowly bent down and on the side of the bed she spotted a pair of red underwear on the floor.

***

Malik reentered his dorm room. Malik looked around the room, but saw no one.

"Aniya?" Malik shouted. He walked further into the room when he noticed his cellphone on the floor. He bent down to get it when he saw the pair of red underwear on the floor.

"Dammit," Malik swore as he rose up from the floor, his cellphone in his hand. He rushed out of the room, hollering for Aniya down the hall. Everyone was looking at Malik like he was crazy.

Aniya was sitting against the side of the building crying.

"Oh God, I can't take any more, please! I just miss my momma! I need my momma!" Aniya cried out loud as tears steadily poured down her face. "Why must I go through this? I'm hurting, and I'm hurting bad! I wish I would die already—nobody wants me anyway!"

A hand gently touched Aniya's shoulder. Aniya slowly looked up, her vision blurry. She couldn't clearly see who was in front of her.

"You poor child, you must not give up so easily. God never put more on us than we can bear," a voice said.

Aniya tried to wipe her eyes, but the tears wouldn't stop.

"Remember, prayer changes all my dear," said the voice.

Aniya just sniffed.

"Give me your hand, child. You don't need to be hanging out here like this, it could be dangerous."

Aniya raised out her hand toward the figure.

The lady took Aniya's hand and placed money in it.

"Take a bus back home. There's no need for you to be on these streets," the lady said as she helped Aniya off the ground. "The worst may be near, but the best has yet to come." She wrapped her arms around Aniya.

Malik was running outside screaming for Aniya. Aniya was getting on a bus that had stopped across from the dorm. Malik ran to the street when the bus passed right in front him.

***

Night was falling when Aniya finally made it home.

The bus let Aniya off on a corner close by Nancy's house. It got darker as Aniya walked alone, rubbing her arms to warm herself up. Aniya turned the corner when she saw cop cars surrounding Nancy's house with their lights flashing. Neighbors were surrounding the area as well.

"Oh God, what is going on?" Aniya whispered to herself.

Aniya walked through the crowd and spotted Nancy crying with her husband holding her. A cop was writing on a notepad while others were talking to some neighbors.

"What's going on?" Aniya asked a lady in the crowd.

"I think someone's young girl is missing," she said, not even looking at Aniya.

"Nancy!" Aniya screamed as she ran through the crowd, holding her belly with one hand.

Nancy slowly raised her head off her husband's shoulder as she noticed Aniya running in her direction.

"Aniya," Nancy whispered, looking at her as if she saw a ghost. "Aniya!"

Nancy ran to Aniya and hugged her tightly as she continued to cry.

"Nancy, what's going on?" Aniya asked as she pulled away from the hug.

"Baby, I was worried sick. No one knew where you were," Nancy explained as she looked Aniya in the face, holding her arms tightly.

Jeff walked up to Aniya and Nancy and said, "Aniya, baby, are you okay?"

"I'm fine," Aniya said softly.

"Okay, everyone. Clear the area," the police shouted to the crowd.

***

Later that night, Nancy slowly opened Aniya's door.

The room was filled with darkness. Nancy crept up by Aniya's side and stood over her with an evil glare, breathing heavily. Nancy slowly removed the cover off Aniya's belly. She began to gently rub Aniya's pregnant belly.

Aniya slowly turned her head in Nancy's direction, slowly waking up. Nancy whispered, "You're going to be just fine Aniya. Because you will never leave this house again."

Aniya's eyes slowly opened as she tried to get a word out.

"Shhhhhh," Nancy hushed as she slowly stuck a needle in Aniya's arm.

Aniya tried to speak, but nothing came out of her mouth. Everything went blurry. Nancy removed the needle and Aniya's eyes then shut completely. Nancy threw the needle on the floor and pulled out a knife.

"I'm sorry, Aniya, but you just don't listen. Things like this can happen when you try to leave with my child," Nancy said as she raised the knife in the air.

***

Malik and his class entered a rehab facility and began looking around strangely at their surroundings. The teacher cleared her throat to make an announcement.

"Okay class, take this facility seriously and make some good observations. This project is worth 300 points. Remember, you are free to ask questions to the staff on duty. Learn as much as you can about certain people and take notes on why they're here and how would you diagnosis them. However, if someone wants to stay confidential, please do not pressure anyone for any information. This facility was nice enough to let us have a hand on experience for this particular class. Is that understood?"

Everyone bowed their heads and some mumbled the word, "Understood."

"Okay everyone, split up and let's get this on a ball," said the teacher as she snapped her fingers in the air.

Malik was coming from the restroom, busy fixing his shirt, when he bumped into someone.

"Oh, excuse me," said Malik as he looked up.

Malik continued to stare in silence.

"Malik, is that you?" asked Anita as she pushed her hair behind her ear.

"Ms. Anita, you look amazing," said Malik as if Anita just took his breath away.

"Well thank you," said Anita as she put her head down in shyly, swinging her leg from side to side.

"I don't know what to say," said Malik as he took short breaths between his sentences as she raised his hands in the air.

"You don't have to say anything," said Anita as she turned in the opposite direction. "I wasn't expecting to run into you here. Is there someone you know here?"

"No, I'm here on a school assignment," he said as he scratched his head.

Silence filled the hallway.

"You care to sit with me a while?" Anita asked as she turned back to face Malik.

"Sure," Malik responded as he put out his hand for Anita to lead the way.

Anita sipped her cup of coffee.

"So, this your new spot?" said Malik as he tried to lighten the mood with a smile.

Anita placed her coffee cup on the end table. "For the time being. Once I'm well I will be free to leave," responded Anita as she sat back and crossed her legs.

"Well, it looks like you're on your way. I'm glad to see you doing better," said Malik as he rubbed his two hands together.

Anita dug in bra and pulled out a pack of cigarettes. She began to hit the bottom of the pack and a cigarette popped to the top. She threw the pack of cigarettes on to the coffee table and lit one.

She took a long puff of her cigarette. "So, how are you and my daughter?" Anita asked as she blew the smoke from her mouth.

Malik took a slight pause and rubbed his head. "To tell you the truth, Ms. Anita, my first time seeing her was yesterday."

"What?" Anita said as she removed the cigarette from her lips. "You haven't seen my daughter since after you got her pregnant."

"It was a total misunderstanding," Ms. Anita. I thought she didn't want anything to do with me. She never reached out to me and Nancy said---"Malik was cut off by Anita.

Anita rose up. "That Nancy is a no good woman. I felt something bad about her from the first time I laid eyes on her."

Anita walked up to Malik and put her hands on each of his arms. "Promise me one thing," she said.

"What's that," Ms. Anita?" Malik asked as he stared into her eyes.

"See about my child before something horrible happens to her," she pleaded as a tear drifted down her cheek.

The next day at Malik's house, his mother was in the kitchen making lunch when her mother stepped in.

"Hi, baby," Silva said as she kissed Sandra on the cheek.

"Hi, momma. I see you are up from your nap."

"A well needed one indeed."

"Why don't you take a seat at the table and I'll fix you some coffee."

"Thanks, honey," Silva said as she took a seat at the table and began reading the newspaper.

There was a loud bang at the front door. It scared Sandra so badly that she dropped the knife she was cutting her vegetables with. Malik's grandmother quickly took off her reading glasses and put her newspaper down. Sandra and Silva both looked at each other with confused expressions on their faces.

The banging continued. Sandra quickly ran to the door along with Silva. Sandra opened the door and Craig busted through it.

"Craig, what in the hell is your problem? Why are you busting into my house?" Sandra shouts as she placed her hand on her hip.

"Where is Malik?" Craig yelled, looking around the room.

"My child is not here and you need to get the hell out of my house!"

Craig started pushing Sandra to get her out of the way. She started screaming as Silva grabbed a huge umbrella that was by the door and started whacking Craig with it.

Malik's sister, Coretta, came running from upstairs.

"What's going on?" she yelled when she saw the scene in her kitchen.

"Woman, I have a right to know where Malik is! I haven't seen Anita or Aniya since I went to jail!" Craig shouted at Sandra.

"Keep you and your troubles away from my son!" she yelled back.

"If you don't get out of here right now, I'm going to whack you again!" Silva shouted.

"Listen, I don't care about you or the trash you call a family. My son is in college doing just fine without y'all bothering him," Sandra said as she pushed on Craig once more.

"Yea, leave my brother out of your mess! You a no-count man! That's what you are," Coretta said.

Craig walked up to Coretta and glared at her.

"Get away from my child!" Sandra demanded as she pulled on Craig's arm.

Craig yanked his arm back.

"If you touch her, I will kill you!" Silva yelled as she held the umbrella high in the air.

"You don't scare me one bit!" Coretta said to Craig said as she folded her arms.

It got quiet for a while as Craig breathed heavily. A moment later, Malik opened the front door without anyone hearing him.

"It's my blood that runs through that child's veins, and as long as Malik is living I will have dealings with him when I want," Craig said as he pushed Coretta back. Hearing the commotion, Malik ran into the kitchen.

"Hey, keep your hands off my sister!" Malik shouted as he rushed at Craig.

Craig and Malik began to throw punches at each other. Everyone was screaming as Sandra and sister tried to break the fight apart.

"If you don't stop it now, I will call the cops!" Silva shouted as she began to dial 911.

Sandra and Coretta finally pulled the two men off of each other. Malik's nose was dripping blood and Craig wiped blood from his lips. They stared at each other in rage. Malik slowly reached in his pants, pulled out a gun, and pointed it at Craig.

"My God! My God, put that gun away! It's not worth it, Malik!" his mother shouts.

"And to think I cared for this. Go ahead, shoot the man who gave you life," Craig said as he stepped forward into the gun.

"Ma, what's this jerk talking about?" Malik asked his mother, never taking his eyes off of Craig.

"Yeah, go ahead Mrs. Goodie-Two-Shoes. Tell him who kept a roof over his head, kept him dressed, put food in his mouth," Craig said while his chest heaved against the gun.

"You ain't nothing to me!" Malik said angrily, pressing the gun harder against Craig's chest.

"This has to stop now! God doesn't like family against family. There is no respect for our elders!" Malik's grandma shouted. "Now Malik, you put that gun away. Since when did you become a thug packing a gun?"

"Malik! Honey!" Sandra said as she began to cry. "I'm so sorry, baby! I didn't mean to keep this from you."

Malik slowly put down the gun; disbelief on his face. The gun hit the floor. Malik grabbed his head with his hands as he turned around, knocking over the bookshelf on the wall.

Sandra screamed.

"Malik! Now, now, baby. I know you're hurting, but listen to grandma! Healing takes time," Silva said to him.

"I'm sure momma was thinking she was doing what was right. He's a scumbag!" Coretta shouted.

Malik stormed out of the house, slamming the door behind him.

"My God! My God, how much more can I take?" Malik cried as he hit the ground, falling on his knees.

"Malik!" cried his mother as she ran to his side.

"God, we need you more than anything. Lord, after the storm comes the rainbow. I know you can bring this family back to peace and love. God, have mercy on our souls!" Malik's grandma said as she raised her hands to the heavens.

***

Later on that evening, Malik parked his car in front Nancy's home.

He knocked on the door and Nancy answered. She stood in complete shock without saying a word.

"Hi," Malik said nervously as he fidgeted with his fingers.

Nancy still didn't say a word.

"I was wondering if I could speak to Aniya? If it's possible?"

Nancy still didn't say a word as she breathed heavily.

"It's important," Malik continued as he cleared his throat.

"I'm afraid she's in no mood to talk to anyone," Nancy replied as she folded her arms.

"Would you please tell her I'm here?" Malik pleaded as he put his hands together.

"Now, why would I lie?" Nancy said as she started to close the door in Malik's face. "You're going to leave my property." Malik stopped the door with his hand.

"Not until I talk to Aniya!" he demanded as he took another step.

"Do we have a problem here?" Jeff asked as he walked up behind Nancy. He looked at Malik and folded his arms.

Nancy backed away from the door as Malik took a deep, frustrated breath.

"Look, man, I just want to see my girl!" he said to Jeff.

"Well, your girl doesn't want to see you. You're the reason she's in the predicament she's in now! From what I heard, you don't think the baby is yours. So what do you want?" Jeff said.

Malik just stared at Jeff.

"Don't come back to my door again or we will have a problem!" Jeff said before he slammed the door in Malik's face.

Malik left the house and walked back to his car. Jeff watched Malik from the window.

"Honey, are you all right?" asked Jeff as he walked over to rub his wife's arms up and down.

"Yeah, I'm fine," Nancy said as she leaned her head down to rest on her husband's chest.

Malik got to his car, but as he got ready to stick his keys in the door, he looked back up at Nancy's home. Malik crept back into Nancy's yard and went around to the back of her house. He heard a loud cry come from within the home. He moved to an open window to peek in. The room only had a little lamp illuminating it.

The cry got louder.

"Aniya?" Malik said as he moved from side to side to see if he could get a better look inside. He spotted her in the room. "Aniya!"

All of a sudden, Aniya's door opened slowly. Malik got down to where no one could see him, but he could still see inside. Nancy was doing something to Aniya, but Malik couldn't tell what it was. Aniya began to scream more.

"Aniya, would you stop this unnecessary noise?" Nancy shouted as Aniya became suddenly silent. "Now, that's a good girl."

Malik sneezed and Nancy's eyes widened as she turned quickly to look out the window. She spotted no one. She then closed the window and dropped down the blinds as Malik took off running to his car.

Nancy returned to the front door to make sure Malik had left. As Malik's car pulled off, Jeff appeared behind Nancy.

"That boy is the reason Aniya keeps hurting herself. Jeff, we can't let Aniya hurt this baby—we just can't!" Nancy said as she turned to him and let tears rolls from her eyes.

Jeff hugged Nancy tight as Nancy raised an eyebrow.

Malik parked up the road and called the cops. He gave the police Nancy's address and told them a girl was being abused. As soon as he hung up, his phone rang. He answered it immediately.

"Malik, where are you? I'm getting worried!" said the voice on the other line.

"Momma, I'm waiting on the cops!" Malik said, his voice trembling.

"Malik, where are you?" his mother asked again.

Cop cars flew past Malik, their lights flashing and their sirens blaring. Malik turned his car around and followed them. The cops jumped out of their cars, and so did Malik. The cops banged on Nancy's door.

"Open up! It's the police!" shouted one of the policemen.

Jeff opened the door, looking confused and worried at the same time.

"I'm sorry, can I help you?" he asked politely.

"May we take a look inside? There's been a report that someone may be getting abused at this residence," said one of the officers.

"I'm sorry, there must be a mistake. We seem to have no problems here," Jeff said.

"Sir, may we take a look?" the officer repeats.

"Excuse me, what's going on here?" Nancy said while closing her robe.

"They're saying they want to come in because there has been a report of abuse," Jeff told her.

"Well, that's pretty funny to me. I'm his wife and, if I do say so, I look perfectly stunning," Nancy said, giving the officers a light laugh and a smile.

The cops look puzzled.

"Ask her about the girl that's in that house," Malik said as he stepped up angrily behind the police. Nancy and Jeff stared at Malik in silence.

"May we step inside?" the officers repeated again.

"Sure," Nancy said with a fake smile on her face. "Come on in."

It was very dark throughout the house.

"You and your wife will go to jail for what y'all did to my girl," Malik said as he folded his arms.

"Some talk coming from a hood rat," Jeff said under his breath. The police were monitoring the house outside looked back and forth at both of the men.

"A hood rat?" Malik said, offended.

"You don't want anything to do with the mother of your child. You disowned your child before she was even born," Jeff said as he glared at Malik.

The police continued to search through the house as the men argued by the front door.

"Besides, you should thank us for caring and loving Aniya. She has a mother on drugs! She's only a teen and is about to have a baby by a chump like you. This better be the last time I catch you around here or there will be hell to pay," Jeff said.

Aniya was sound asleep in her bed, lying peacefully.

Clean sheets that were pearly white were covering her body. The room was neat and clean with relaxing music coming from the radio.

"You see, I told you she was in great hands," Nancy said to the police officers.

"Turn on the light, ma'am," said one of the policemen.

Nancy hit the light switch and the officers took a closer look. Nancy noticed the needle on the floor by the side of Aniya's bed.

At the front door, Malik and Jeff continued to argue.

"If you want applause for what you do, that's fine with me. You only do things for show. Neither you nor your wife give a rat's ass about

Aniya. Your wife only wants a baby. She is using Aniya to get what she wants. If you don't get your wife help now, you will both be in jail for a very long time. And guess what? You can't wear your fancy suits and call the shots in there," Malik said.

Back in Aniya's room, Nancy secretly kicked the needle under the bed and said, "You see? She's in good hands, officers."

"Sorry for the trouble," said one of the cops. One of the officers bent down by the bed with his flashlight. Nancy began to breathe faster.

"Oh, look ma'am," said the officer as he picked up the needle. "Someone could hurt themselves."

Nancy let out a sigh of relief and said, "Thank you, officer."

Outside, Sandra pulled up and jumped out of her car. She ran into Nancy's yard.

Nancy and the officers all stepped outside to find Jeff, Malik, and Sandra.

"It's best that you keep your troubled son away from my home! Next time I will have him put behind bars. He can forget about that little scholarship he got. Do you understand?" Nancy said as she pointed directly at Sandra.

"You little wench! Let me tell you something!" Sandra said as she pushed Malik out the way. "You mess with my son and I promise you, you will have trouble on your hands. Do you understand me?" she said as she got in Nancy's face.

"Get these pathetic people out of my yard and away from my wife!" Jeff said to the police.

The officers ordered Malik and his mom to leave the yard.

Everyone left as Nancy crept back into Aniya's room. She turned on the light as she grabbed the bloodied sheets from under the bed.

"You rookie cops," Nancy muttered as she placed the sheets in a bag. She turned off the lights and closed the door.

Malik and his mom made it home and entered the living room quietly. Silva was sitting in a rocking chair, rocking back and forth.

"Oh, momma, you scared me! What are you still doing up?" Sandra asked her.

"I was worried about the two of you," Silva said.

Malik flopped down onto the sofa and took a deep breath.

"Are you okay, son?" Silva asked him.

Sandra placed her purse and keys on the coffee table and took a seat on the sofa.

"No, grandma. I'm not okay," he said as he put both hands on his head.

"You know, God is a healer. He knows how to restore," Silva said as she rubbed her hand on Malik's.

"Well, I don't know how he's going to fix this one. I don't even know the woman who's supposed to be my mom!" he started. "I just found out my daddy is nothing but a drug dealer and an abuser. And I can't even do what it takes to help out my own girl! My girl, who's carrying my unborn child! I feel like I have failed at life. I should just give up!"

His mother spoke up and said, "Malik, I am the woman who raised you. I did the best I could. Yes, I may have had secrets from you, but I thought it was in your best interest."

Silva looked at Malik and said, "You know, when people reach their lowest, that's when God is the closest. I'm not speaking up for your momma, but I know the power of God. Sometimes he uses bad situations to bring families close together. Maybe that's the reason for all this. But in the end, the Devil loses and we are shaped into the people God wants us to be—you just watch."

Chapter Nine

The next day, Sandra parked across the street from Nancy's home. She watched as Nancy pulled out of her driveway.

As Nancy passed her car, Sandra ducked down out of sight. Nancy stared suspiciously at the car. Once Nancy drove off, Sandra immediately stepped out of the car.

She ran across the street and knocked on Nancy's door. She looked around and knocked once more. No one answered.

"Malik, you're lucky I love you and that I need your forgiveness!" Sandra said to herself. She crept around Nancy's house, looking through the windows. Suddenly, she heard a noise coming from one of the windows. Sandra peered in and noticed someone moving around, groaning in pain.

Sandra leaned up to take a closer look. It was Aniya.

"Aniya, honey!" shouted Sandra through the crack in the window.

Aniya turned her head to the window.

"Help me!" Aniya said as tears rolled down her face. She was in excruciating pain.

"Oh God, Aniya, baby!" she said, covering her mouth when she saw Aniya raise a bloodied hand toward her. "How do I get you out of there?"

"Go to the front of the house! There's a key in the mailbox, please hurry! I think I'm losing my baby!" Aniya cried.

Sandra took off running to the front of the house. She got the key out of the mailbox, unaware she was being watched by an old man who lived next door. She then rushed through the house as she called out for Aniya.

"In here!" Aniya said breathlessly.

Sandra barged into the room, letting out a scream when she saw Aniya. Aniya had her hand over a cut on her stomach, trying to keep any more blood from coming out. Sandra noticed Aniya getting dizzy. She put an arm around Aniya and helped her get out the house.

"Will I die?" Aniya asked as she looked over at Sandra. A tear fell down her cheek.

"Aniya, I won't let that happen! I promise!"

The neighbor that had been watching walked up to Sandra and Aniya.

"Well, don't just stand there! Help us!" Sandra screamed at him.

The man helped Sandra put Aniya in the car and closed the door.

"Sir, you need to call the police. Your neighbor just attempted murder."

Sandra pulled off as she put on her hazard lights.

Nancy drove past Sandra on the street and quickly parked in her driveway. She got out of the car and she saw her neighbor staring at her. She put her purse on her shoulder and headed toward her house.

"Hi, Mr. Thomas! How are you today?" Nancy said with a pleasant smile.

He just stared at her.

Nancy turned and walked toward her house, confused by his expression. She turned around to say something else to him, but he had disappeared. She entered her home and went straight to Aniya's room.

But Nancy saw no one. Blood stains were left on the carpet and things were knocked over onto the floor. Nancy gasped for air.

"Oh no," Nancy said as she placed her hand over her heart. "Aniya! Aniya!" Nancy ran through the house, searching through rooms and closets for Aniya. There was no trace of Aniya.

Nancy went to the front door and noticed that police cars were pulling up to her house, surrounding her yard. Nancy quickly closed the door before anyone saw her.

***

"Give her oxygen!" shouted one nurse. "IV going in!" said another as Aniya was rushed into emergency surgery. Sandra reached for Aniya before the nurses held her back. She was not allowed in the operating room.

Sandra was pacing back and forth in the lobby when a doctor came out from the double doors.

"Ma'am," said the doctor. Sandra quickly turned around.

"Yes, doctor?" she said as she walked up to him. "Oh God, tell me she's all right."

"She's fine," he said. "She had to go through emergency surgery to have the baby due to the loss of blood. If she waited any longer she may have died, along with her child."

"Oh God, the baby," whispered Sandra as she placed her hand over her heart.

"The baby is fine, just a little early. We are still running tests on her."

"Oh God, can I see her? Can I see Aniya?"

"Yes, but she's in recovery at the moment. May I ask you a few questions about this young lady?" the doctor asked.

At that moment, some police officers walked into the lobby.

"I think we need to do the same," said a policeman as he walked up to Sandra and the doctor.

***

Sandra entered Aniya's hospital room as Aniya slowly began to open her eyes.

"Hey Aniya, how are you feeling?" Sandra asked softly as she held Aniya's hand, rubbing it gently.

"Is my baby okay?" Aniya asked in a tired voice.

"Your baby is just fine," Sandra replied as a tear fell down her face.

"Can I see her?"

Sandra took a deep breath.

"What's wrong?" asked Aniya.

"Aniya, can I ask you something?"

"Sure."

"Aniya, would you do anything to hurt you or your child? And I want an honest answer."

Aniya slowly removed her hand from Sandra's hand and said, "How could you ask me such a thing?"

"Aniya, Nancy talked to the police and said you tried to hurt yourself," Sandra explained.

"What? I would never do such a thing!" she explained. Aniya silently shook her head from side to side.

"Aniya, what is it? What happened in that house?" Sandra asked as tears flowed from her eyes.

"To tell you the truth, I don't remember what happened. But I know I would never hurt my child. I believe Nancy wants my child!"

The police entered the room as Aniya looked up. Sandra turned to look at them as they came through the door.

"Tell them everything, Aniya," she said.

***

The next morning, Aniya slowly opened her eyes and saw Malik sitting in the chair beside her hospital bed. He was holding her baby.

"Malik," Aniya said softly. He looked up at her and smiled.

"Rise and shine, mommy," Malik said as he stood up with the child to stand beside Aniya. "How are you feeling?"

"She's beautiful," Aniya said as she began to cry.

"She looks just like you," Malik said. "Aniya, you're going to make yourself sick. Here, you want to hold her?"

"Yes," Aniya said as she wiped the tears from her eyes.

Aniya held her arms open to receive the child. Once she was in her arms, Aniya kissed her baby on the forehead.

"You're going to make a great mommy," Malik said as he rubbed Aniya's hair.

"How can you be so sure? I'm already off to a bad start. I'm young, I have no roof over my head, I have no job, I'm in the 11th grade, and I have a psycho woman that's trying to take my child. Do you need me to go on, Malik?"

"I'm here now," Malik said.

"No, you're not," Aniya said.

"What are you talking about Aniya?"

"I know, Malik. I know about Shania."

Malik took a deep breath while staring at Aniya.

"She means nothing," he said.

"Don't. She had to mean something. You still have relations with her," Aniya said. Malik lowered his head.

"Malik, there's something I have to tell you," Aniya said.

"Wait! Before you do, I have a surprise for you," Malik said. He left the room and came back quickly with Anita right behind him.

"Mom!" Aniya cried.

"Baby, oh my baby," Anita said as she rushed over to Aniya's side. "Oh baby, I'm sorry I couldn't be here with you." Tears flowed from Anita's eyes as she hugged Aniya tightly.

"Oh momma, I'm so glad to see you," Aniya cried into the hug.

"I missed you so much," Anita said.

"I missed you too, mommy. I know you might not believe me, but for a long time I didn't know you wrote to me."

"It's okay baby. I'm just happy that you are away from that evil lady. I told you, Aniya, I didn't like something about her," Anita said. "Oh Gosh, let me hold this angel!" She reached for the baby.

Sandra entered the room a moment later along with Coretta. They had balloons and gifts for the baby.

"Hello, everyone," Sandra said.

"Hey, mom," Malik said as he went over to his mother and gave her a hug.

"Hi," Aniya said.

Anita and Sandra stared at each other for a second.

"Anita," Sandra said.

"Hi," Anita responded.

"I got you these flowers," Malik's sister said to Aniya.

"Thank you," Aniya said.

"May I hold her?" asked Sandra.

"Sure," Aniya said.

"Oh, she is just the most gorgeous baby I've ever seen!" Sandra cooed.

"Hey, I'm your auntie, baby," Malik's sister said as she kissed the baby's hand.

"You see, I told you everything was going to be just fine. We're going to be all right," Malik whispered to Aniya as he held and kissed Aniya's hand.

A nurse knocked on the door before entering it with papers on a clip board.

"Hello, everyone," she said as she stepped into the room, closing the door behind her. "How are you feeling, sweetie?" She walked over to Aniya's side and Malik took a step back to make room.

"I'm okay, I guess," Aniya said.

Anita went to the other side of Aniya's bed and kissed Aniya on the forehead.

"I love you baby," she said.

"Well, I'm Jennifer," said the nurse. She rubbed Aniya's arm. "Okay, parents. I just need you to sign the birth certificate and I'll be out the way."

The nurse handed the clipboard to Aniya. Aniya hesitated and bit her lip.

"Well, sometime today so daddy can sign!" Malik said jokingly.

Aniya signed the birth certificate and ignored what Malik said. She then handed the clipboard back to the nurse as a tear rolled down her face.

"Aniya, are you okay?" the nurse asked.

"I'm sure she will be fine. This is all just new to her, that's all," Anita said.

"Whether we like it or not Aniya, we are all family now. We will do our best to help you and my son with this precious baby," Sandra said as she rubbed Aniya's arm up and down.

"Yea, and I'll babysit," Coretta said.

Malik took the clipboard from the nurse. But as the pen hit the paper, Aniya spoke up, "Malik, don't sign that birth certificate."

Everyone looked at her in astonishment. There was complete silence.

"Aniya, what are you talking about?" Malik asked.

Malik's sister let go of the baby's hand as she stared at Aniya.

"Don't sign the birth certificate," Aniya repeated, not looking in his direction.

"Aniya, what's going on?" Anita asked.

"I heard you the first time, Aniya. But what do you mean?" Malik asked with a deeper tone to his voice.

Sandra spoke up, "Aniya, are you saying—"

"I'm saying, Malik," Aniya said as she looked at his face. "You might not be the father." Tears began to fall down her face.

"You're not for real!" Malik said in denial.

"My child is not the father?" Sandra repeated.

"Aniya, there was someone else?" Anita asked.

Aniya started to cry heavier than before.

"It's okay, baby. We can do a DNA test if you like," said the nurse.

"You're damn right we will do one!" Malik shouted as he threw the clipboard down on the ground. "I can't believe this shit! Aniya, you looked me dead in the eye and swore this was my baby!"

The baby started crying.

"Everyone, calm down. Let me just take the baby to the nursery and I'll get someone to bring papers for the DNA testing," the nurse said before taking the baby.

Aniya was still crying hysterically.

"You should be crying! You hurt a lot of people!" Sandra said.

"Now, you just back off of my child! Malik shouldn't have been having sex with my daughter in the first place!" Anita said, defending Aniya.

"It's probably some thug's from the streets," Sandra said as she shook her finger at Aniya.

"Damn," Malik said as put both hands on his head. "Aniya, I love you—how could you cheat on me? How could you find the time? We were always together!"

"It's okay, baby, I will help you—you don't have to cry," Anita said to Aniya.

"Momma, I don't want to hurt you," Aniya said between sobs.

"Oh baby, I love you so much. I will be by your side no matter what!" Anita said while hugging Aniya as she lay in the hospital bed.

"Momma, you won't understand," Aniya said as she looked into her mom's eyes.

"Of course I will, sweetie."

"Momma, I was raped around the same time I slept with Malik!" Aniya cried.

"What? Aniya, what are you talking about?" Anita shouted, standing back from her daughter.

"Aniya, by who?" Malik shouted.

"That's what they all scream when they sleep around one too many times!" Sandra said as she folded her arms.

"Malik, don't believe her! She's nothing but trouble!" Coretta added.

"Would you shut your brat up?" Anita shouted at Sandra.

"As soon as you shut up your slut!" Sandra shouted back as she stood.

"That's it! You've done it now!" Anita said as she reached to hit Sandra. Malik stepped in the middle and stopped them from fighting.

"Mom!" Aniya cried.

A couple of nurses entered the room.

"Is everything all right in here?" said one of the nurses.

"Yes, everything is fine," Malik said.

"If there's any more commotion in here, we will ask everyone to leave," said the other nurse.

"Understood," Malik said.

The nurses left the room.

"Tell me who did this. I swear I will kill him!" Malik said to Aniya.

"Baby, go ahead so we can put this jerk behind bars," Anita added.

***

It got quiet for a second.

"I'm out of here," Sandra said, breaking the silence.

As soon as Sandra touched the handle of the door, Aniya let it out.

"Craig," she said, keeping her eyes down.

"Craig?" Anita asked, shocked.

"What? Craig?" Sandra asked as she turned back to Aniya.

"Oh, mommy. Please don't get mad at me! I didn't want to hurt you, momma!" Aniya cried more.

"Oh God!" Anita shouted as she fell to the floor, landing on her knees.

"He's mine," Malik said angrily as he walked out of the hospital room. Tears steadily flowed from Sandra's eyes as she left the hospital room with her daughter right behind her, following after Malik.

"Malik, where are you going?" his mother shouted as they walked out of the hospital building.

"I'm going to kill him, mom! I swear I will kill him!" Malik shouted in rage as he continued to run.

***

Night fell.

"You know, Jeff," Nancy said as she brushed her hair at the mirror in her room.

"What is it, honey?" Jeff asked as he lowered his glasses while reading the paper in bed.

"I think you should take that position your job offered you," she said while continuing to brush her hair.

Jeff snickered and said, "You have to be kidding, right?"

Nancy put her brush down and quickly turned to Jeff with a very serious look on her face.

Jeff looked at his wife and put his paper down before he continued, "What? You was all against us moving and now all of a sudden it's okay?" asked Jeff, confused as he took his glasses off his face.

Nancy knelt next to the bed by Jeff.

"Jeff, the truth of the matter is that they aren't going to give Aniya her baby back. They believe she's a threat. After the police finish this investigation, that baby will belong to us." I don't want to have any more confusion around us. Just peace. That's all.

"What?" Jeff asked as he sat up straighter.

"But Nancy, that's not our child. You're talking like you're insane!" Jeff said as he rose off of the bed.

"Maybe not yet, but soon she will be," Nancy said with a grin.

Jeff just shook his head in awe as he ran his fingers through his hair. He paced back and forth.

"Nancy, it's been nothing but trouble since we welcomed this girl into our home. Now you want to deal with the baby too?" Jeff said as he stopped pacing and stared at Nancy.

"What if I promise there will be no more trouble from her?" Nancy said.

Jeff and Nancy stared at each other as silence took over the room.

***

The next day at the hospital, Malik was getting swabbed for the DNA test.

Malik entered the hospital room as Aniya was getting up off the bed. He caught her by the arm as she stumbled back onto the bed.

"Let me go, Malik! I don't need your help," Aniya said as she stood up.

"Aniya, listen," Malik said. "I'm sorry about acting out of line! You're the one who really endured so much tragedy. I'm sorry. I wish I could have protected you."

Aniya started to cry as Malik wrapped his arms around her.

A nurse entered the room.

Aniya slowly raised her head from Malik's chest.

"I know this is a difficult time and a very difficult situation," said the nurse. "The good news is you get to go home. The bad news is that the baby has to stay due to you having her so early. We need to make sure she's healthy before she leaves the hospital."

"I have to leave my baby?" Aniya cried.

"You can see your baby as much as you want, Aniya. She will be fine," the nurse assured her.

***

Saturday night fell.

Rain was pouring heavily and lighting covered the sky as thunder roared. The hospital was busier than ever. In the nursery, new babies were being put to sleep while others were crying or being fed.

Nancy entered the hospital with stolen scrubs and a face mask on. She looked around before she walked swiftly past the emergency room doors. She pressed the button to the elevator. When the doors opened, a doctor walked into the elevator with her.

"Do you work here?" The doctor asked her, trying to make conversation.

"Uh, yes. I mean, no," Nancy said nervously.

"Is that a yes or a no?" he asked sternly.

"Yes, I'm new to this hospital. I'm on call to any hospital in the area," Nancy said.

"Are you sick?"

"Excuse me?"

"Why is your face covered?

"I guess I just have a little cold," Nancy said.

The elevator opened and the doctor stepped out as Nancy looked up at him.

Nancy hit the button for floor 8. Once the doors opened, she exited the elevator. She looked down the hall both ways and saw a pregnant woman down the hall. The woman could barely walk without her husband helping her. On the other side of the hall, a nurse was walking with a baby, patting him on the back.

Nancy walked up to the nursery room's glass window. She stared at the babies, placing her hands on the glass.

"Excuse me, may I help you?" a nurse asked Nancy.

"Yes, I'm here to help in this department," Nancy said, her face still covered by the mask.

The nurse raised an eyebrow at Nancy.

"Oh, uh," Nancy said as she removed the facemask.

"May I have your name? I'll check the roster." the nurse said.

"Uh, Judy," Nancy lied nervously.

"Judy who?" the nurse asked impatiently.

"Judy Hargrave," Nancy said.

"Is she our help?" another nurse asked. She was standing in the doorway of the nursery. She looked exhausted as she rocked a crying baby in her arms.

"Yes, I'll go make sure she's on the roster. Also, you're needed immediately in room 806. Mrs. Shelly is having another one of her episodes," she said to the other nurse.

"Okay," the nurse said to Nancy. "You can get acquainted with the little ones and I'll be back shortly."

Nancy walked into the open door of the nursery.

"Just grab a baby and keep it quiet!" said a nurse that was inside the nursery.

Nancy gave her a shy smile as she looked at all the babies.

"They won't bite, trust me," the nurse added with a smile.

"They're just all so adorable," Nancy said.

"We're so shorthanded, we're grateful for your help."

A baby girl began to cry in the corner.

Nancy slowly walked up to the baby.

"Oh, she's tiny," Nancy said.

"Yeah, a young girl had her. They are saying she tried to cut the baby out. I mean, she looks like such a psychopath. I mean, she denied doing it, said some woman by the name of Nancy did this to her. Who knows? The cops are investigating," the nurse explained.

"May I hold her?" Nancy asked as she rubbed the baby's arm.

"Sure, that's what you're here for," said the nurse. "Be gentle with her, she came a little too early."

Nancy picked up the baby and held her in her arms.

"What's her name?" Nancy asked as she stared into the baby's eyes.

"Lilrie," said the nurse.

Nancy's head rose slowly as she stared at the wall with a tear falling down her face.

"Lilrie," Nancy whispered.

"Are you okay?"

"Yea, yea I'm fine."

"Good. It looks like all the babies are settling down, so I'll step outside for just a sec," said the nurse. "Will you be okay?"

Nancy nodded, holding the baby tightly.

***

A while later, the head nurse entered the nursery.

"Okay, Judy, I don't see you on the roster," she said as she looked up from her clipboard.

Another nurse walked in behind her.

The head nurse turned around and asked, "Where's Judy?"

"She's right over—" the nurse trailed off when she noticed no one was in the nursery. "Oh God, she can't be far! She has the new baby, Lilrie!"

"She's a fake, we have no Judy Hargrave! She just stole the baby! Call for a code red!" the head nurse shouted.

Nancy ran down the hall with the baby covered up as a doctor turned the corner and walked toward her. Nancy opened a door and entered an empty room. She placed the baby down on an empty bed. She took the scrubs off and let her hair loose. She picked the baby up again and quickly went out the back entrance of the hospital.

She walked into the rain. As she started to walk away, someone tapped her shoulder.

***

On Sunday morning, Anita was sitting in church before everyone one else got there. She was crying when the preacher stepped into the sanctuary.

"What troubles you, my child?" asked the preacher as he walked up to Anita.

Anita slowly looked up as she wiped the tears from her eyes.

"Anita, is that you?" he asked.

"Yes, it's me, Preacher. It's been a long time hasn't it?" she said. "I thought you might have forgotten me."

"Oh, of course not, my child. I have prayed for you daily," he said as he took a seat by Anita, rubbing her on her back. "I knew that one day, God would bring you back."

"My world is shattering right before my eyes. I don't know how much more I can take."

"Anita, have you ever seen a rainbow after a storm?"

Anita looked up at the preacher.

"Yes," she replied as she sniffled.

"We don't see that rainbow unless the storm happens. God will never put more on us than we can bear Anita. Sometimes, the hardships we are dealt carry a message. They make us a better person—a stronger person. Never give up on God. He'll never give up on you," he said before kissing Anita on the forehead. The preacher then stood and began to walk away.

"Preacher?" she called out as she ran over to hug him tightly. "Thanks."

The preacher hugged Anita gently.

"God has you now, Anita. All you need to do is continue to follow him."

"Malik, how do you know she didn't set this up? Besides, she never told you about being raped because she probably wasn't," said Shania as she stood in front of Malik. He sat on his bed with his hands placed under his chin.

"Look, now is not the time, Shania. I don't buy anything you're saying," he said as he tried brushing her off.

"I saw the way that man Craig and Aniya were interacting with each other. You really think she wanted that baby Malik? How could you believe anything she says or does after she exposed her pregnancy to everyone at your mom's Job?"

Silence filled the room as Malik slowly raised his head. "What did you just say?"

"I said she doesn't deserve you, Malik," she said as she backed away slowly.

Malik rose from the bed with anger in his eyes. "How did you know about that?" he yelled. "Besides, Aniya never knew where my mom worked."

Shania began taking deep breaths. "Malik," she whispered.

"Shania," Malik started. "You bring so much trouble in my life. The best thing is for you to leave this very moment and never return."

"But Malik, I love you. I know you love me too," said Shania as she reached her arms out to him.

"Get out," Malik shouted as he pushed Shania into his dresser. "I never want to see you again."

***

"No!" Aniya shouted as she hit the floor. She was in the hospital, surrounded by cops, doctors, and nurses while Malik was kneeling on the floor next to her, holding her.

"Where's my baby? Where's my baby? Where's my baby?" Aniya cried in agony.

***

Shaquana Jackson

Dear diary,

I haven't written in a while. It's just that too many things have been happening in my life. I felt there was no reason to live. I live in an apartment complex in the projects where anything can go down at any given time. My mom has spent most of her life on drugs. Even I, her child, could not change her. For days at a time I never saw my mother. Sometimes she disappeared without warning. Drugs will have you do anything, no matter who you hurt in the process. Sometimes I couldn't focus because of hunger pains. Sometimes I didn't know when I would have anything to eat again. Different men were always in our home. The guy who gave her drugs raped me. He got her hooked so that he could have his way with me. I got pregnant by a guy who has a prosperous future—or at least, that's what I thought. Because the rape, it was too close to know who the daddy really was. Then, the most precious thing in my life was taken away from me. It's like someone ripped my heart out and stepped on it. My daughter is in danger somewhere. She is not in the midst of all this love with her family. My mom almost went back to drugs—thank God she didn't. My mom and Malik's mom learned to get along for their granddaughter and the sake of their kids. Oh, and by the way, the test results came back. Malik is the father. Malik's mom and I have become close and the truth came out about the embarrassing notes left at Malik's mom's job. It wasn't me. It was hard trying to shake things back together without the blessing that holds our family together, my daughter, Lilrie. It's been over year today...

Oh God, you never fail me. I will get my baby back. We haven't stopped looking.

***

There was a knock on Aniya's bedroom door. She quickly took her diary and put it under her pillow.

"Come in."

"Hey, are you ready for work? I figured we could get a head start. It's so hot out there!" Anita said. Aniya just kept her head down.

"Baby, what is it?" Anita said as she stepped into the room. She walked over to Aniya.

"Oh, mom, I don't want to do anything! I'm tired of trying. I just want to give up!" Aniya cried.

Anita took a seat beside Aniya and put her arms around her.

"Aniya, you have preached to momma, prayed for momma, and stuck by momma. You have been my rock for so long and there's no way I'm going to let you give up—especially when you've come so far. Baby, you have two weeks before graduation. You've done everything that you needed to get our baby back. Continued with your education, got a job along with your momma— even though it's at a burger joint. You put our money together so we can pay a private detective to get your baby back. "You know Nancy and Jeff got pull with the police because her father was a detective for many years. He then moved up to Mayor. The police don't want to take this seriously." And what about Malik and his family? Think about what it will do to them if you don't follow through, Aniya. I love you so much," Anita said as she hugged her daughter tightly, rocking back and forth.

***

Anita and Aniya were walking down the sidewalk holding hands.

"Thanks, mommy," Aniya said.

"For what?" Anita replied.

"For encouraging me and being my rock."

"Hey, there's no need to thank me. I put you through enough and you still love me," Anita said, smiling.

A car blew the horn as it pulled beside Anita and Aniya.

"Hey girls, need a lift?" Sandra called out.

"Hey, thanks! Great!" Anita said as they got into the car.

Sandra drove them to the burger joint that they worked at. Anita and Aniya thanked her as they began stepping out of the car.

"Aniya," Sandra said as she turned around, placing her hand on top of Aniya's.

There was silence as Aniya and Sandra looked at each other.

"If there's anything you need, please let me know, okay?"

Aniya gave her a shy smile and stepped out of the car.

***

"Rock a bye, baby, on the tree top. When the wind blows, the cradle will rock," Nancy sang as she rocked back and forth in her rocking chair.

The rug with Lilrie's name was in the middle of the nursery. Pictures of Lilrie, Nancy, and Jeff were hanging on the purple painted wall.

"Momma's baby forever," said Nancy as she rubbed Lilrie's face.

"What is it, sweetie? Mommy loves you so much," Nancy said. "It's time for bed." She placed Lilrie in her white crib laced with purple trimmings. Nancy put on the nightlight beside the crib.

Someone watched Nancy secretly through the window.

Nancy kissed Lilrie on the forehead and shut the door, leaving it open a crack.

Nancy was in the shower when Jeff entered the bathroom.

He heard Nancy crying and pulled the shower curtain back.

"Honey what's wrong?" he asked her.

"I don't know. It's just that things have been too good lately. I just have this feeling that I'm going to lose our daughter," Nancy said.

"Oh, Nancy. I didn't say anything for a while but I think we should give her back. If Aniya was trying to harm her baby like you say, maybe they will give her back to us," Jeff said before he kissed her.

"Are you crazy? We'll never see her again," Nancy said as she wiped her nose.

If we don't give her back we may be in more trouble than we can think. We may never get her back, said Jeff as he rose up.

Nancy watched Jeff walk off as tears steadily flowed down her face.

***

The next morning, Nancy entered the nursery. Lilrie was standing in her crib biting on her teether.

"Hey, baby," Nancy said as she picked Lilrie up from the crib, bouncing her in her arms. Lilrie laughed as Nancy began kissing her.

"Where's your favorite stuffed animal?" Nancy said as she reached into Lilrie's crib. She noticed a piece of paper folded in half in the crib.

Nancy slowly reached for the paper and opened it up. It read:

In due time, that baby will be with her real mother.

"No!" Nancy shouted as she began running through the house with Lilrie in her arms. Nancy opened the front door when she ran into her husband.

"Whoa, whoa! Where are you flying to like that?" Jeff said as he held Nancy back.

"Someone was in the house! They were around our child!" cried Nancy.

"Nancy, what are you talking about?" he asked. Nancy showed Jeff the paper and the baby began to cry. "Okay, Nancy. Let' just get back in the house."

Nancy backed up into the house with the baby as Jeff entered after her.

"Okay, you just stay put. I'll check things out," Jeff said.

Jeff entered the back of the home slowly, walking the dark hall. Jeff heard a noise from within Lilrie's room. When he entered, he heard another noise from the window. He slowly walked to the window, looking outside.

A man was standing in the back of the yard, smoking a cigar. The man stared at Jeff as Jeff stared back at him.

"Hey, get out of my yard before I call the cops!" Jeff called out to him.

Meanwhile, the baby was still crying while Nancy tried to fix Lilrie some milk.

"Hey, did you hear what I said?" Jeff yelled, getting angrier by the minute. "Do you want me to come out there and kick your ass?"

The man grinned as he turned and walked away, flicking his cigar to the ground.

"Honey?" Nancy said as she walked in to the nursery and tapped Jeff on his shoulder. Jeff jumped and quickly turned around.

"Who were you talking to?" Nancy asked.

"Uh, no one," Jeff said nervously. "Where's the baby?"

"She's in her high chair in the kitchen," Nancy said. Jeff stayed silent for a moment. "Jeff, what is it?"

Jeff took off to the kitchen with Nancy right behind him.

"Jeff, talk to me!" she cried.

Jeff picked up Lilrie out of her high chair. "I think someone is after us," Jeff said.

Silence filled the kitchen.

"Someone just may be here for Lilrie, Nancy," said Jeff as he took his glasses off his face.

"I'm going to call the cops!" Nancy said as she reached for the phone.

Jeff said to Nancy calmly. "What are you going to tell the cops? That you stole someone's baby and now they're coming back for her?"

It got quiet as Nancy began to breathe harder.

"Oh gosh," Nancy said as she placed a hand over her heart and put the phone down with her other hand. "Jeff, we have to do something!"

***

There was a knock on the door. When Aniya answered it, she saw Malik standing there with flowers. She gave him a big smile.

"Hey, beautiful," Malik said.

"Malik! Hi," Aniya said. They hugged tightly. "It's so good to see you."

Aniya and Malik entered Aniya's room.

"What's the occasion?" Aniya said, putting the flowers on her dresser.

"Excuse me?" Malik said as he took a seat on the bed.

"You brought me flowers."

"You deserve so much more," he said as he pulled Aniya to him, sitting her on his lap. Aniya put her head down sadly.

"What's wrong?" he asked her.

"Will we ever get her back?" she asked softly.

Silence took over the room.

"Aniya, where's your faith?" Malik asked. "Remember when she first got taken from us? You didn't believe you would ever go back to school or get a job. But you did both. Your mom is completely free of drugs, my mom is closer to you and your mom, and your mom got a job along with you. "We all pitched in to help pay for the private investigator since Nancy's father is Mayor and has pull with the police. Aniya, no matter how you look at this, God is moving and knows that everything happens for a reason."

"I just can't believe it's been almost two years," Aniya said.

"We will have our little Lilrie back, I promise."

***

Nancy was looking up and down her street as she placed Lilrie in her cartoon car seat. A guy was seated in a car across the street, looking at her through binoculars. Nancy got in her car and pulled off, passing in front of the row brick homes. The man put his binoculars down and ducked his head low as Nancy zoomed past him.

A man walked up and approached the car.

"I need this process to speed up," the man said, the man in the car jumped.

"Damn, Craig! You scared the shit out of me! And yes, I understand!"

"No, I don't believe you do, detective," Craig said as he reached in his coat pocket. He pulled out a stack of money and threw it in the car, letting it fall on the detective's lap. "Two more days until her graduation. I need that baby placed in my son's arms, do I make myself clear?"

The detective nodded his head as he looked into Craig's eyes. "Craig," said the detective. "Why are you doing this?" Craig slowly turned around as he fixed his suit coat. "I've been diagnosed with cancer," he replied.

"Craig, I had no idea, man. I'm lost for words," said the detective.

"It's quite alright. I don't have long left, so I just want to make things right before I go."

"Craig, don't talk like you're going to give up," said the detective as he shook his head.

"Thanks for not getting the cops involved even though you know that I'm wanted. However, when this is all said and done, you may turn me in," said Craig as he backed up and walked away from the car.

***

It was graduation day.

Aniya was in her room, putting on her graduation gown, when she heard a knock on her bedroom door.

"Come in!" she called.

"Hey, baby," Anita said as she entered Aniya's room.

Aniya turned from the mirror to her mom.

"Hey, mom," she said as she gave her mom a small smile.

"You look so gorgeous!" Anita said as tears rushed from her eyes.

"Mom," Aniya said, blushing as she quickly walked up to her mom and hugged her.

"I'm so proud of you!"

"Thank you, mom, for everything."

***

Cops pulled up to Nancy's driveway. Some police surrounded the house as they pulled out their guns. The police moved into the house and put both Nancy and Jeff in handcuffs.

"Nancy, it looks like your father couldn't help you with this one. You're going in for a long time for abducting a child," said one of the officers.

***

Malik's mom pulled up to Aniya's house and knocked on the door. Aniya ran down the steps to answer the door.

"Oh, baby, you are so gorgeous!" she said to Aniya.

"Thank you," Aniya responded.

"May I have a hug?"

"Of course," Aniya said as she hugged Sandra.

Anita smiled, watching from behind Aniya.

***

The detective was sitting outside Malik's home. Malik came out, locking the door behind him. The detective stood outside of his car.

"Malik," called the detective. Malik looked at the man with a confused look.

"Excuse me, but do I know you?" asked Malik as he began to approach the detective.

"I believe I have someone who belongs to you," he said as he unbuckled Lilrie out of the car seat and handed her to Malik. Malik's tears flowed steadily down his face and Craig watched the reunion from afar.

***

"Where's Malik?" Aniya asked his mother.

"He told me he had something to take care of, but he will make it in time," Sandra said.

"Are y'all ready?" Anita asked.

Aniya looked back at her mom and said, "I couldn't be more ready."

Chapter Ten

At graduation, the students were taking their seats, getting ready to receive their diplomas.

"Welcome, everyone, to a very special occasion," said the principal into the microphone. Aniya kept looking back to see if she could see Malik in the crowd.

"May all the graduates stand?" the principal continued.

The music began to play, marking the start of the ceremony. Anita and Sandra both smiled at Aniya as she stood. The passing of the diplomas began.

"Shirley Captaville," the principal said as she gave Shirley her diploma with a handshake. Aniya bit her lips as a tear fell from her face.

"Aniya Cooper," said the principal. It was like everything began to flow in slow motion. Aniya stepped on stage and looked back to the audience for the last time.

When she did, she almost lost her balance.

"My baby," she whispered. "My baby!" Aniya watched as Malik held her daughter, walking down the aisle toward her.

Aniya took off running as everyone stood to see what was going on. Aniya took her baby from Malik and hugged her tight, weeping.

Anita, Sandra, and his sister surrounded Aniya and Malik.

***

Dear Diary,

This is the happiest day of my life.

My daughter is back and my family is complete. I graduated, my mom is doing awesome, and Malik just got drafted into one of the best football teams ever! Malik is saving up to buy a house so we can be the family we were meant to be.

God knows in my heart how much hatred I have for Craig. However, I heard he was the reason my daughter was returned to me. I pray that one day I can forgive him for all the horrific things he put my mom and I through.

My mom also has a nice new man in her life now.

As I write I'm watching my daughter be rocked too sleep by her dad.

Thank you God!

www.ingramcontent.com/pod-product-compliance
Lightning Source LLC
Chambersburg PA
CBHW050639300426
44112CB00012B/1864